S0-ABZ-843

THE LIQUIDITY STRUCTURE
OF FIRMS
AND MONETARY ECONOMICS
by William J. Frazer, Jr.

University of Florida Monographs

SOCIAL SCIENCES
No. 27, Summer 1965

UNIVERSITY OF FLORIDA PRESS / GAINESVILLE, FLORIDA

PREFACE

This essay was an outgrowth of a number of articles in the general area of the liquidity of firms and monetary economics. Some of the articles were my own. The preparation of the essay was motivated, in part, by correspondence with William H. White, International Monetary Fund, and by discussions with Montgomery D. Anderson, University of Florida. Both made helpful comments leading me to believe that a longer and more detailed treatment of some of my work was called for. In Dr. White's view, this longer treatment was apparently to emphasize my use of statistics and the significance of my results for several topics in monetary economics.

The results presently reported involve a large number of regression equations relative to the standards of an earlier time. Without the modern computer, the task of generating these equations would have been virtually impossible for a fully employed, un-supported college teacher. For the present writer, too, this essay would have been impossible without the assistance on the computer of Mary Ann Frazer, in particular, and of Bert Davis. Moreover, an anonymous reader for the University of Florida Press and one of my former professors—Arthur F. Burns—had some impact on the final outcome of the essay. Professor William S. Vickrey was instrumental in having me take a second look at the first article discussed in Chapter 5.

I wish, further, to express appreciation to Dale L. Moody, computer laboratory, College of Business Administration, University of Florida, and William Levin, Chief, Division of Financial Statistics, Federal Trade Commission, and the National Science Foundation. Mr. Moody checked the computer results. Mr. Levin and one of his colleagues read the section on the FTC-SEC data. A part of the final editing and rewriting was done during my tenure as a "Science Faculty Fellow," the National Science Foundation. Publication was made possible by the Graduate School of the University of Florida.

All of those mentioned above are absolved from any responsibility for the commissions contained in the essay and for omissions.

WILLIAM J. FRAZER, JR.

SECANE, PENNSYLVANIA
MARCH, 1965

CONTENTS

1. INTRODUCTION

A number of topics in monetary economics concern the liquidity structure of firms and accounts determining the liquidity structure such as those for cash, government securities, and bank loans. These topics include the motives of holding money (Secs. 3.1, 7.1, and 8.1), commercial loan doctrine (Chap. 4), the income velocity of money and near moneyness (Sec. 5.2), trade credit and monetary policy (Chap. 6), wealth and the income velocity of money (Chap. 7), and factors affecting the postwar rise in the velocity of money in the United States (Chap. 8). This essay deals with the liquidity structure of firms and these topics, and the results of numerous statistical analyses of data concerning them.

The essay is a part of a growing literature that deals with firms in terms of their impact on aggregates for the economy as a whole. Such aggregates would include those for income, output, expenditures, the average of prices, and the turnover of money balances. Often even individual firms as a part of a sample, or firms by asset size classes (or industry groups), will be studied with the view to improving our understanding and/or predictions of the behavior of the aggregates and the effects of changes in general credit conditions. The studies, consequently, possess elements of both micro- and macro-economics: the former to the extent that small units or samples of units by asset size are involved; the latter to the extent that a connective link is established between the parts and the whole, or to the extent that results contribute to an understanding or better prediction of the behavior of the aggregates and the effects of general credit conditions.

In this literature there are recent articles dealing with the liquidity aspects of firms by Allan H. Meltzer, Alan W. Heston, Ernest Bloch, Lawrence S. Ritter, Richard T. Selden, and myself, among others.[1] Some of the works are almost entirely empirical—Heston's, for example. He deals

---

1. Meltzer, "Mercantile Credit, Monetary Policy, and Size of Firms," *Review of Economics and Statistics*, Nov., 1960; "Monetary Policy and the Trade Credit Practices of Business Firms," *Stabilization Policies* (Englewood Cliffs: Prentice-Hall, 1963), pp. 471-97. Heston, "An Empirical Study of Cash, Securities and Other Current Accounts of Large Corporations," *Yale Economic Essays*, Spring, 1962. Bloch, "Short Cycles in Corporate Demand for Government Securities and Cash," *American Economic Review*, Dec., 1963. Ritter, "The Structure of Financial Markets, Income Velocity, and the Effectiveness of Monetary Policy," *Schweizerische Zeitschrift für Volkswirtschaft und Statistik*, Sept., 1962. Selden, "The Postwar Rise in the Velocity of Money: A Sectoral Analysis," *Journal of Finance*, Dec., 1961. Frazer, "The Financial Structure of Manufacturing Corporations and the Demand for Money: Some Empirical Findings," *Journal of Political Economy*, April, 1964; "Monetary Analysis and the Postwar Rise in the Velocity of Money in the United States," *Schweizerische Zeitschrift für Volkswirtschaft und Statistik*, Dec., 1964; and see references in the cited works.

primarily with annual data from balance sheets and income statements for 209 firms. Bloch's work, too, is largely empirical: his data are from the sources drawn upon in this work (Sec. 1.2). Ritter, on the other hand, presents some analysis of liquidity and approaches it from the viewpoint of developments in the financial markets. My own work most nearly resembles some aspects of Meltzer's, in terms of approach and sources of data (Chap. 6), although Meltzer has, in addition, dealt with a special sample of 86 firms. In a variety of respects my work either complements or conflicts with various elements of the work of others, as some subsequent chapters reveal. These, however, should serve as a means of highlighting similarities and areas of agreement and disagreement.

The major contributions of this essay are developed mostly in Chapters 3, 7, and 8. The questions dealt with in these chapters are listed below (Sec. 1.1), following a brief outline of some analytical foundations of monetary economics. The other contributions are aside from the main ones. They are largely on the negative side and deal with some conflicting notions in the literature on various aspects of the liquidity of firms. The questions dealt with in these chapters, too, are listed below. Various aspects of monetary analysis and the present sources and analyses of data are also introduced (Sec. 1.2).

1.1. ANALYTICAL FOUNDATIONS, THE LIQUIDITY STRUCTURE, AND SOME IMPLICATIONS

The analytical foundations of monetary economics, as presently seen with respect to changes in the liquidity structure of firms, are only briefly outlined in this section. These and certain statements about changes in the liquidity structure of firms are shown to rather loosely suggest inadequacies in prevailing notions of the relationships between certain real, monetary, and financial variables. The analytical foundations and the suggested inadequacies anticipate subsequent topics and tests of data.

An outline of analytical foundations.—Given the axioms concerning rationality and the preference for more assets rather than less, and total assets as a constraint, it may be shown that the flow of returns from holding assets in general is a maximum when the rates of return from the acquisition of additional assets of the various types are equal. Similarly, given the same axioms and some other total for a combination of liabilities or some combination of accounts serving as a source of funds, it may be shown that the cost of obtaining a given amount of funds is a minimum when the rates of interest from obtaining given amounts of additional funds from any of the several sources are equal. Further, given the axioms and proceeding from a condition of equilibrium, it may be shown that a direct change will occur in a given class of assets whenever the rate of

2

return from acquiring additional assets in that class changes, other rates remaining momentarily unchanged.[2] Here we view the flows of returns as including both expected net dollar amounts (i.e., net of all cost except the cost of funds) and psychological returns associated in varying degrees with the convenience and security in holding certain assets.

Now, as firms increase in size, and attributing the optimizing quality (and its dual, economizing, where costs are involved) to their managers (in accordance with our axiom about preference), we can make an additional assumption: some economies in the management of cash result from the use of a stock of liquid securities as a partial substitute for bank loans as a means of effecting adjustments in the need for (or excess of) cash. This we can put in a form that will permit subsequent empirical testing:

ASSUMPTION: *As firms increase in size, the ratio of government securities to bank loans increases.*

For the present, however, we simply state the latter assumption and recall the second aspect of the definition of the precautionary motive for holding cash. The definition, as set forth by Keynes, concerns two types of demand for money:

(type 1) the demand for cash as a proportion of assets (or income) "to provide for contingencies requiring sudden expenditure and for unforeseen opportunities of advantageous purchases . . ."

(type 2) the demand for an asset whose "value is fixed in terms of money to meet a subsequent liability [e.g., bank indebtedness] fixed in terms of money. . . ."[3]

We shall be concerned with only the second type of demand until Chapter 7. Thus, given the assumption about government securities, the above analysis, and the second part of the definition of the precautionary motive, we may state a principal proposition:

PROPOSITION: ". . . *the precautionary demand* [*of type* 2] *does not increase proportionally with wealth* (*or total assets in the present instance*) *as wealth rises, and presumably income with it*" (italics added).[4]

For instance, as firms increase in size, the ratio (as a percentage) of government securities to bank loans increases. This parallels a weakening of the precautionary motive relative to the other motives—the transactions and speculative motives—as defined elsewhere,[5] and we expect cash to decline as a proportion of assets. Thus, we have a corollary to the principal proposition:

2. See Frazer and William P. Yohe, *Introduction to the Analytics and Institutions of Money and Banking* (Princeton: Van Nostrand, 1965), Secs. 4.1, 17.4.

3. *The General Theory of Employment, Interest and Money* (New York: Harcourt, Brace, 1936), pp. 195-97, 170-71.

4. Frazer, "Financial Structure," p. 177.

5. Frazer and Yohe, Sec. 2.2

COROLLARY: *The turnover of cash balances increases as firms increase in size beyond some minimum size (as defined in Sec. 7.2).*

In this instance, balances affected by the precautionary motive, in effect, get drawn into the more active transactions sphere as firms increase in size. Here the change in the turnover of balances would be indicated by some substitute measure for the income velocity of money (i.e., the ratio of income to the stock of money) such as the ratio of sales to cash.

All the above changes affect liquidity, broadly defined as

$$\text{liquidity} = \frac{\text{cash} + \text{government securities}[6]}{\text{total current liabilities}}$$

or, as an index of near moneyness

$$\text{near moneyness} = \frac{\text{government securities}}{\text{total bank loans}}$$

The latter is of special significance. It is involved in an above assumption, and it may be related to the corollary to the principal proposition in view of the role of asset size in both the assumption and the corollary. The index also focuses more exclusively than the liquidity ratio on the accounts (Sec. 2.2), other than money, that are most likely to reflect the firms' demands for liquidity or, more specifically, near moneyness. The accounts involving trade credit are largely determined by the size of operations (Secs. 6.2, 2.1), and tax liabilities are determined by profits and the tax laws. In both instances—liquidity and near moneyness—the left-hand members of the expressions are a decreasing function of bank indebtedness, and this contribution of bank indebtedness to "immoneyness" has been referred to as a "neglected factor" in analyses of the demand for money.[7]

To determine whether tests of data are consistent with the principal proposition, data concerning statements of relationships are tested and the results of the tests are reported later. These statements include:

1. Corporate liquidity is directly related to asset size.
2. Government securities as a percentage of assets is directly related to asset size.
3. Cash as a percentage of assets is inversely related to asset size.
4. Total bank borrowing as a percentage of assets is inversely related to asset size.
5. Cash plus government securities as a percentage of assets is independent of asset size.
6. The ratio of accounts receivable to accounts payable is independent of asset size.

Later, too, the corollary to the principal proposition is shown to be consistent with tests of data.

6. Frazer, "Financial Structure," p. 177; this liquidity ratio is also used in Meltzer's work on trade credit: "Mercantile Credit," p. 430, and "Monetary Policy," p. 476.

7. See Richard H. Timberlake, Jr., "The Stock of Money and Money Substitutes," *Southern Economic Journal*, Jan., 1964, p. 255.

4

Questions anticipating subsequent topics.—As revealed by the outline of analytical foundations, the major contributions of this essay concern firms' demands for money, the portion of the precautionary motive dealing with the relationship between cash and firms' indebtedness at the bank, liquidity or near moneyness, and the turnover of firms' balances. In connection with these contributions, we deal with questions such as: whether the index of near moneyness is an important determinant of the turnover of firms' balances, whether there are economies (Sec. 7.2) in the management of cash by larger firms, whether the precautionary motive (Secs. 3.1, 7.1) affects the demand for money, whether the precautionary motive reveals any previously neglected factors, whether the latter have affected the postwar rise in the velocity of money (Sec. 8.1), and whether differences in the near moneyness of firms by asset size indicate a need to distinguish between the routes by which credit conditions exercise their effects on firms by asset size (Secs. 7.2, 8.1).

Other less obvious questions concern some possibly conflicting notions or approaches in the literature on various aspects of the liquidity of firms. For one set of such questions, we may ask whether bank loans to manufacturing corporations are a major source of funds for the purchase of inventories, whether the ratio of bank loans to business inventories is relatively independent of asset size, or whether there is a strong possibility of stabilizing inventory purchases by stabilizing bank loans to manufacturing corporations as revealed by the relationship between changes in inventories and changes in bank loans. We might also ask if government security holdings are simply related to tax liabilities, or if there is "a near perfect intra-year coordination of changes in tax liabilities and of government holdings" for classes of manufacturing corporations with assets below 100 million dollars as some maintain.[8] And, finally, we may question whether bank credit to large firms gets redistributed to smaller firms within the corporate manufacturing sector by increases in net receivables (i.e., accounts receivable less accounts payable).

1.2. Notes on Monetary Analysis and the Sources and Analyses of Data

The data and the form in which they appear for firms by asset size seem, in some respects, to be ideally suited for the present approach. Their appearance in absolute amounts as well as in percentages of total assets, for example, lends itself readily to the use of analytical notions about changes in scale and constant proportions, and it suggests a use of linear approximations to relationships concerning cross section data for firms by asset size. There are some special problems, on the other hand,

8. Bloch, pp. 1059-62.

concerning the selection of input values for class intervals, the selection of an upper bound for the largest class of firms, and other matters. This section deals with these problems as well as with other introductory matters pertaining to monetary analysis, and the sources and analyses of data.[9]

The data.—The data used in the present study are primarily those reported by the Federal Trade Commission (FTC) and the Securities and Exchange Commission (SEC) in the *Quarterly Financial Report for Manufacturing Corporations*. The FTC-SEC report provides balance sheet and income statement information and their data appear for firms classified by asset size, as well as according to the standard industrial classification. The data are said to be based on a sample from among those firms filing United States corporate income tax forms 1120, but they include, in fact, a complete canvass of all corporate manufacturers with assets of 5 million dollars and more.

The data for firms by asset size or industry group are in (or may be reduced to) a percentage form such as bank loans as a percentage of assets or retained earnings as a percentage of net income (after or before federal income taxes). This feature means that the operating and financial characteristics of the respective industries and asset size groups are reduced to so-called common size statements or measures independent of the number of firms or the amount of assets per se in each group. To illustrate the feature's significance, one may think of a given asset size group, with assets distributed in given proportions. Now, let us double the total and all categories of assets or, for that matter, let us vary the scale of operation by any multiple. What then is the effect of the change in the size per se on the initially given asset distribution? Quite simply, of course, there is no effect. But the point is important. It means that amounts expressed as percentages of total assets are independent of the dollar volume of assets in various asset size classes. A study of the percentages or selected ratios (expressed as percentages) in relation to asset size, consequently, may reveal structural changes that take place as firms increase in size rather than the simple alteration of the total amount of assets accounted for by any asset size group.

Class intervals.—The classes of firms considered in most instances in-

9. A note on the uses of the term "analysis": (1) One use refers to the part of mathematics that involves algebra and calculus methods; (2) another refers to the arrangement and interpretation of materials ostensibly dealing with real-world phenomena—in this instance one may be concerned with the explicit or implicit use of mathematics and/or theoretical constructions in economics as tools; (3) another use refers to the fitting of a curve (or line) to a sample of observations, each of which consists of specific values for two or more variables, as in regression analysis. In this essay, the term is used in both the second and third instances. In the latter, the term is often used in the plural. This usage indicates that lines have been fitted to cross section or time series data for classes of firms.

6

clude (in millions of dollars): Under 1, 1 to 5, 5 to 10, 10 to 25, 25 to 50, 50 to 100, 100 to 250, 250 to 1,000, 1,000 and over. In the statistical analyses the mid-points (denoted X_1, X_2, . . . X_9) of the class intervals have been used, partly because of their simplicity and use in preliminary research and partly because of some inadequacies in the data required for calculating the mean values for the class intervals.[10] A special problem arises, however, in the selection of the mid-point of the class interval for firms of 1,000 million dollars in assets and over, where asset size enters as the independent variable. Here an upper bound of 2,000 million dollars was selected so that the resulting class interval would contain the greatest frequency of firms over the years for which data are tested.[11]

Some other characteristics of the data.—Other characteristics of the data calling for special consideration include the following: The FTC-SEC's use of a blow-up of amounts from a sample of financial reports for firms under 5 million dollars, and the practice of determining annually the size class for a given firm. In the first instance, the blown-up sample is in lieu of a complete canvass of firms such as that used for firms with 5 million

10. The mean values would seem appropriate on theoretical grounds. Even so, the mid-points are satisfactory for use in the present approximations to true relationships in view of the relatively small differences between the mid-points and the corresponding mean values for the various class intervals. The mid-points and some mean values for selected dates are shown in the table (dollar amounts in millions).

CLASS INTERVAL	MID-POINTS OF CLASS INTERVALS	MEAN VALUES FOR THE 1ST QUARTER OF 1959	MEAN VALUES FOR THE 1ST QUARTER OF 1963
Under 1	.5	(†)	(†)
1 to 5	3.0	(†)	(†)
5 to 10	7.5	8.38	8.38
10 to 25	17.5	15.88	15.43
25 to 50	37.5	35.39	34.48
50 to 100	75.0	70.42	71.11
100 to 250	175.0	160.25	156.14
250 to 1,000	625.0	525.73	504.27
1,000 and over	1,500.0‡	2,550.29	2,501.81

†The data for firms under 5 million in assets are from a blown-up sample. They do not provide the information for calculating the mean.
‡Assumes an upper bound of 2,000 (see next note).

11. To help in setting this bound, the Fortune Directory for large firms was consulted (see, e.g., "The Fortune Directory: The 500 Largest U.S. Industrial Corporations," *Fortune*, July, 1963, pp. 177-96). The information reported to the Directory indicated that an upper bound of 2,000 million dollars (and thus an input value $X_1 = 1,500$ million dollars) was adequate. Of the 27 manufacturing firms reported in the 1963 Directory as having assets over 1,000 million dollars for example, 19 were contained in the 1,000 to 2,000 million dollar class interval. The 27 firms included such exceptionally large firms as General Motors, Ford Motor Company, U. S. Steel, DuPont (E.I.) deNemours, and a few others. Due allowance for the size of these firms and for distribution of the firms in the class interval 1,000 million and over, however, would lead one to exclude these firms in calculating any input value. Such allowance would likely result in a value of about 1,500 million dollars, but it need not imply that the exceptionally large firms should be excluded in effecting linear approximations to data.

dollars and more in assets. It means that precise quantitative interpretations are more difficult to make for the class of firms with assets below 5 million dollars. With respect to the latter of the above characteristics, a firm may increase sufficiently in asset size to fall in a higher class during a given year, but the reclassification occurs annually and it may cause shifts in the absolute amounts for the various accounts shown in the FTC-SEC's *Quarterly Financial Report*. This practice of reclassifying the firms after the year's end imparts a possible bias that renders the absolute amounts somewhat deficient for use as time series. The possible bias, however, could have only minimal effects in some instances. As evidenced above in note 11, firms by asset size are fairly evenly distributed within the classes used in the present analyses, although the FTC's Division of Financial Statistics reports a tendency for more than half of the number of corporations in an asset size class to be in the lower half of the class when asset size classes are further broken down. Even so, where the various amounts for accounts as percentages of assets are used, the bias from a shift in absolute amounts is likely to be minimized since the percentages are "independent of the number of firms or the amount of assets per se in each group." In addition, where analyses of data concern the relationship between two accounts such as bank loans and inventories, both accounts are somewhat similarly affected by the possible changes in the classification of firms. These comments do not dispose of the potential shortcomings of the FTC-SEC data for certain purposes. They do indicate, nevertheless, that conclusions based on the analysis of the data as absolute amounts and as time series should be stated most tentatively, and that cross section analyses of the data are likely to be favored as a means of avoiding the most deficient aspects of the data, especially in those instances where observations of asset size enter the analyses.

Finally, the FTC-SEC increased the number of classes for reporting data on firms by asset size from seven to nine in the fourth quarter of 1956. This was the result of dividing the former top class into three classes. Furthermore, in the first quarter of 1959 they combined the former first two classes into one class and divided the 10 to 50 million dollar class into two classes, with no net change in the number of classes at that time. The increase in the number of classes for the larger portion of the domain over which asset size may be defined, however, means that we have some advantage (Sec. 6.1) over those using data for an earlier period when the classifications were less adequate. It means, too, that analyses of the data of the type presented in this essay were less feasible prior to gaining experience with the data after 1956.

Linear equations, slope parameters, and coefficients of determination.— A set of points, such as those to which lines are fitted, may be denoted

8

(X_1, Y_1), (X_2, Y_2), . . ., (X_9, Y_9) where the X's are the observed independent-variable values, and the Y's are the corresponding dependent-variable values. The elementary equations defining the linear approximations to relationships pertaining to such points are of the form

$$Y = bX + a + e$$

where Y and X are the dependent and independent variables, respectively, and b and a are the slope and intercept parameters, respectively, and e is a random error term.

The results reported in subsequent chapters pertain to slope parameters (i.e., b's) and coefficients of determination (i.e., r^2's).[12] The magnitudes of the slope parameters are usually small, where the dependent and independent variables are small percentages and asset size (in millions of dollars) respectively. However, the present interest is mainly in the magnitudes in relation to one another and whether the slopes are significantly different from zero.

A rationale for linear approximations.—The earlier point about the amounts (as percentages) being independent of the dollar volume of assets and so on is also of some theoretical interest with respect to monetary economics. In particular, this notion of constant percentages in relation to changes in scale is identical to that whereby absolute amounts vary in proportion to the rise in income (and presumably asset size). And, where the latter notion takes the form of a need for the money stock to rise in proportion to the rise in income as a secular matter, it is basic to large areas of monetary economics, and implicit in the activities of the officials of our Federal Reserve System.[13] It would seem, then, that some basis in theory and practice exists for effecting linear approximations to cross section data dealing with the relationships between accounts as percentages of assets and asset size.

Even so, linear approximations to various relationships are used. In some instances, moreover, notably those involving time series, relationships are usually implicitly or explicitly assumed to be linear, or else the concern is with the direction of change rather than its amount. For example, questions arise about whether changes in the government security holdings of firms under 100 million dollars in assets vary directly and in

12. The statistical method used in generating the results involves the correlation of two variables, simple regression analysis, and the estimation of slope parameters by the method of least squares. It is set forth in a variety of texts: readily available ones include Michael J. Brennan, Jr., *Preface to Econometrics: An Introduction to Quantitative Methods in Economics* (Cincinnati: South-Western, 1960), Chap. 19; John E. Freund, *Mathematical Statistics* (Englewood Cliffs: Prentice-Hall, 1962), Chap. 13; J. F. Kenney and E. S. Keeping, *Mathematics of Statistics* (3d ed.; Princeton: Van Nostrand, 1954), Part I, Chap. 15. A comprehensive table for values of use in t-tests may be found in the latter volume.

13. See Frazer and Yohe, *Analytics and Institutions*, Chap. 2, 20.

about the same amount as changes in tax liabilities, or they arise about whether the ratio of government security holdings to bank loans has risen or declined as a secular matter.

In most respects, analysis in this essay is qualitative. That is, it deals with the direction of changes and with whether some changes are more or less than others, as revealed by linear approximations. This is true in the case of many changes over time and cross section changes in relation to asset size. In the latter instances, for example, concern centers upon whether some slope parameters are more or less significant than others, as may be revealed by the use of t-tests of significance (Sec. 3.1).

The present qualitative analysis and results from linear approximations to data provide strong support for some basic propositions, aid in focusing emphasis upon the relevant factors, and point the way for further research and study. The latter would involve an application of statistical and other techniques to more dynamic aspects of firms' demands for money liquidity, and so on. It would draw upon the present results and deal with relationships between selected leading and lagging variables and a multiplicity of factors operating to, at times, reinforce and, at other times, offset each other in their effects.

1.3. SUMMARY

This essay concerns the liquidity structure of firms and some topics in monetary economics—namely, the motives for holding money, commercial loan doctrine, the income velocity of money and near moneyness, trade credit and monetary policy, wealth and income velocity, and the postwar rise in the velocity of money. Moreover, in anticipation of subsequent chapters and the reporting of the results from statistical analyses of data, assumptions and other statements are introduced about various aspects of the liquidity structure of firms and the above topics in monetary economics. The major assumption and analytical results suggest questions to be answered. Does the ratio of government securities to bank loans increase as firms increase in size? Does the precautionary demand for money balances rise less than in proportion to the increase in total assets (and presumably income)? Does the turnover of money balances increase as firms increase in size, beyond some minimum size?

There are also questions on the negative side—that is, in anticipation of some possibly conflicting notions or approaches in the monetary literature. We ask, in anticipation of further answers, questions about such matters as the relationship between bank loans to manufacturing corporations and the purchase of inventories, the relationship between government security holdings and tax liabilities for classes of firms with assets under 100 million dollars, and the prospect of a redistribution of bank credit between firms in the manufacturing sector through changes in net receivables.

The essay is a part of a growing volume of literature that deals with individual firms or firms by asset size in terms of their impact on aggregates for the economy as a whole. It possesses, consequently, elements of both micro- and macro-economics. The former are present to the extent that small units are involved. The latter are present to the extent that connective links are established between the parts and the whole, or to the extent that information results so as to contribute to an understanding and/or better prediction of the behavior of the aggregates and the effects of general credit conditions. The present study, furthermore, is qualitative for the most part. That is, the concern is often with the direction of changes in selected accounts with respect to changes in asset size. Questions arise about some key accounts rising more and others less than in proportion to a rise in asset size. Such structural differences as revealed by diverse movements suggest the presence of possible conflicts with some prevailing notions about special relationships. The structural differences, however, also support the present approach, since it incorporates them as a part of the approach.

The emphasis on a qualitative analysis suggests a general use of linear approximations to various relationships, although in some instances the prevailing notions about relationships between selected accounts call specifically for linear regression analyses. There is, however, a reason for the use of linear approximations as first approximations. Namely, a basic notion underlying a good bit of theory and practice in the area of monetary economics is that stocks of cash, near-cash assets, bank credit, and so on rise (or should rise) roughly in proportion to the rise in income (and presumably asset size). In any event, the termination of the present phase of investigation should raise questions for future study.

The major sources of data for the various analyses are the FTC and the SEC. In many respects the FTC-SEC's *Quarterly Financial Report* presents data in a form that is ideally suited for the present approach. They appear in absolute amounts as well as in percentages of total assets, for example, and the latter form lends itself readily to the use of analytical notions about changes in scale and constant proportions. There are problems, however, pertaining to the selection of input values for firms classified by asset size and the selecting of an upper bound for the largest asset size class in those instances concerning analyses of cross section data. These are dealt with by using the mid-points of class intervals and by setting an upper bound after examining the distribution of firms in the largest asset size class.

Other characteristics of data calling for special consideration include

11

the FTC-SEC's use of a blown up sample of firms' financial reports as a means of presenting financial data for firms with assets below 5 million dollars and the practice of determining the classification for a given firm on an annual basis. These characteristics mean that precise quantitative interpretations are difficult, especially when they involve firms with assets below 5 million in asset size and the analysis of time series data as absolute amounts. Their presence tends to favor cross section analyses of data for accounts as percentages of asset size, especially in those instances where observations for asset size enter the analyses.

The statistical results that are subsequently reported include slope parameters and coefficients of determination. The slope parameters are tested for their significant difference from zero, or one, depending on the case. The present interest, however, is mainly in the significance of some slopes in relation to other possibly more or less significant slopes rather than in their absolute amounts.

2. ACCOUNTING STATEMENTS, LIQUIDITY, AND NEAR MONEYNESS

This chapter reviews some mechanics concerning the use of accounting statements as sources of data. It also reviews these statements in relation to the earlier measures of liquidity and near moneyness (Sec. 1.1) and in relation to the principal means of effecting adjustments in liquidity and in the cash account. It does so, in part, because of the presence of an underlying view of sources and uses of funds in the subsequent examination of the financial structure of manufacturing corporations and the demand for cash, government securities, and bank loans. It does so, further, in anticipation of some critical comments pertaining to certain views in contemporary literature about specific relationships between selected accounts. Professor Bloch, for instance, as late as 1963, views "a near perfect intra-year coordination of changes in tax liabilities and of government holdings" of manufacturing corporations with assets below 100 million dollars;[1] and his analysis is within the context of a sources-and-uses-of-funds framework. In contrast, the view throughout this essay is that all transactions ultimately revolve about the cash account, and that the more immediate non-cash sources of funds for payments for taxes, inventories, and so on pertain to the liquidity structure generally and non-cash liquid assets and bank loans most particularly. In other words, the present approach recognizes a variety of sources of funds and the prospect that some may be used at one time and others at another time, but the emphasis is on both government and similar securities and bank loans as major means

1. "Short Cycles," pp. 1059-62.

12

of effecting adjustments in the cash account, and the relative importance of the two (as indicated, e.g., by the ratio of government securities to bank loans) may vary with respect to asset size.

2.1. SOURCES AND USES OF FUNDS

Data for the sources and distribution of firms' funds may be obtained from balance sheets and income statements. Income statements reveal some of the sources and uses of firms' funds, and a comparison of balance sheets for a given group of firms at the end of a period with those for the firms at the beginning of the period reveals other sources and uses of funds as well as changes in liquidity, near moneyness, and flows of funds to and from the financial markets, including the money, credit, and capital markets. These statements, moreover, reveal the principal alternatives available to business enterprises for obtaining the means for asset expansion and for effecting adjustments in corporate liquidity and the cash account.

The key sources of funds for asset expansion over which the policy-making units of firms may exercise control are the retention of earnings, bank borrowing, other debt financing (such as mortgages and bonds), and external equity financing, whereas the principal means over which management exercises control in effecting liquidity adjustments are changes in cash, the purchase or sale of government securities or other liquid securities, and increases and decreases in bank loans. From among these, changes in government security holdings and bank loans are viewed as the principal means of effecting adjustments in the cash accounts. Other accounts are of interest, such as accrued taxes and accounts payable, but changes in these accounts are less directly subject to managerial control. Tax liabilities are a function of profits and tax laws. Accounts payable are largely a function of the volume of business operations, the practice of taking discounts for the early payment of trade debt, and—possibly at times and to a relatively small extent—the cost of borrowing funds with which to effect the repayment of trade debt before the due date.[2]

In terms of income statements, an inflow of funds results from sales of goods and services net of any changes in the extention of credit to effect the purchase of such sales. This netting then leaves us with a gross inflow to the cash account, and it may in part be offset by a possible variety of outflows. These would include the cost of sales, services, and production such as wages, salaries, interest, rent, and, in a special sense, adjustments to the cash inflow must allow for increases in accounts payable and funds for the depreciation of plant and equipment. In this special sense, accounts payable and depreciation are absorbing the inflow of funds from sales,

2. This practice is dealt with by Meltzer (Sec. 6.2 below), and Heston, "Empirical Study," pp. 124-26.

although ultimately we view them as sources of funds. The result of our netting process thus far, nevertheless, is corporate earnings, and we may view their distribution in the form of a provision for corporate income taxes, and as retained earnings, and dividends. We may also view them after taxes and, in the context of earlier discussion (Sec. 1.2), the ratio of retained earnings to earnings net of taxes may be said to serve as a means of comparing the relative importance of retained earnings for firms in different asset size groups.

Retained earnings appear as a source of funds and an increase in the balance sheet account for earned surplus, and they permit an offset to any drain on cash. Even the corporate income tax payment may be viewed as a decrease in the liability account for accrued taxes, and if the tax is unpaid, then the increase in the tax liability serves as an offset to outflows of cash. In general, any increase (decrease) in an asset account is a use (source) of funds, and any increase (decrease) in the accounts on the liabilities side of the balance sheet is a source (use) of funds. On the two sides of the balance sheet, one views such accounts as in the accompanying diagram.

BALANCE SHEET

Assets	Liabilities
[An increase (a use of funds) and a decrease (a source of funds)]	[An increase (a source of funds) and a decrease (a use of funds)]
Cash[1]	Accounts payable[3]
Near cash, liquid investments (e.g., government and other liquid securities)[2]	Accrued taxes[4]
	Bank loans[5]
	Bonds
Accounts receivable[3]	
Inventories	Net Worth
Plant and Equipment	Capital stock
(net of depreciation)	Earned surplus

1. "Cash" or "money" may be defined for the present purpose as currency plus demand deposits. The balance sheet account for cash, however, may include portions of time deposits and time certificates of deposit.

2. Throughout the essay the term "government securities" is used with reference to government securities and similar types of liquid assets. These may include some municipal securities and possibly some commercial paper. The FTC-SEC (Sec. 1.2) account for U.S. government securities is reported as including tax anticipation bills and non-guaranteed federal agency issues, as well as the "equivalent" of cash on hand. The latter category may include some negotiable certificates of deposit.

3. The accounts in the FTC-SEC reports most nearly corresponding to the present Accounts receivable and Accounts payable, respectively, are "Other notes and accounts receivable (net)" and "Trade accounts and notes payable."

4. The account in the FTC-SEC reports most nearly corresponding to "Accrued taxes" is "Federal income taxes accrued."

5. The FTC-SEC reports three classes of liabilities for bank loans: short-term loans from banks (original maturity of 1 year or less), installments on long-term debt due in 1 year or less, and long-term debt due in more than 1 year. Term and other types of bank loans would be reflected in these classes of bank loans.

In the case of depreciation, an increase in depreciation is a source of funds, since it is an offset to an increase in plant and equipment or a use of funds.

There are many inflows and outflows of funds, and these serve to some extent as offsets to each other in such a way as to minimize the actual

14

increase or decrease in the cash account from one statement date to another. In effect, all flows may be viewed as going through the cash account, but all of them do not literally represent a change in its magnitude. Some netting out takes place before the flows reflect increases or decreases in cash, and some flows have a larger effect on cash than others. Among the more routine flows, there are inflows and outflows, and the optimizing manager of the cash account should employ any increases in cash in a profitable alternative such as government securities or the repayment of bank loans. He should also make adjustments in these holdings or borrow from the bank if the cash account goes below some minimum working balance.

Among the less routine flows through cash are those involving financial planning for large capital expenditures and those reflecting shifts in the preferences of managers for liquidity. In the former instance, corporate liquidity may be built up from a variety of sources in anticipation of expenditures.[3] Here, cash may be permitted to increase from retained earnings, depreciation, the sale of new stock issues, or some varying combination of debt and equity financing, and these cash proceeds may be temporarily employed in the purchase of liquid securities, the repayment of bank loans, and so on in order to achieve a financial structure capable of providing subsequent means of payment on short notice. In the latter instance, the liquidity ratio may vary in response to shifts in the demand for assets such as cash and near cash assets vis-à-vis those such as plant, equipment, and inventories.[4] In this instance and in the case of a relatively stronger preference for assets with a fixed claim against future income, the build up in liquidity is more likely to result entirely or almost entirely from internal sources.

In both of the above instances, nevertheless, the respective sets of changes may, at times, vary directly and, at other times, reinforce one another.[5] For example, in the early stages of an expansion in economic activity, there may be a weakening in the demand for cash and near-cash assets in relation to bank loans and inventories (in part, as revealed by an increase in the turnover of cash), but the potential decline in the demand for cash and near-cash assets vis-à-vis inventories and bank loans may in part be offset by the preference for liquidity as a future source of funds for carrying out planned capital outlays (Sec. 3.3.); and, approaching a decline in economic activity,[6] and/or immediately following an upper

3. See Frazer, "Financial Structure," pp. 180-82.
4. See Frazer, "Some Comments on Professor Ritter's Interpretations of Keynes and Changes in Income Velocity," *Schweizerische Zeitschrift für Volkswirtschaft und Statistik*, March, 1963, pp. 76-78.
5. Frazer, and Yohe, *Analytics and Institutions*, Sec. 17.2.
6. The term "economic activity" suggests activity such as the hours of work, the

turning point, a strengthening of the demand for cash and near-cash assets in relation to bank loans and inventories may be reinforced by a decline in the need for liquidity as a pool of funds for effecting future capital outlays.

2.2. LIQUIDITY, NEAR MONEYNESS, AND THE PRINCIPAL MEANS OF EFFECTING LIQUIDITY AND CASH ADJUSTMENTS

The net result of some of the above changes may be indicated by the liquidity ratio and the index of near moneyness, both as set forth earlier (Sec. 1.1). The magnitude of the liquidity ratio, especially with reference to the magnitude of the numerator (or the denominator), is important as an indicator of the capacity of enterprise to effect expenditures on short notice, and it is one indicator that managers may focus upon in attempting an optimal utilization of financial resources. But, for the present purposes, both the liquidity ratio and that for near moneyness are important as means of dealing with possible differences in the capacity of different asset size groups to effect expenditures or cash adjustments on short notice, all in relation to asset size and independently of the dollar volume of assets in any given asset size group (Sec. 1.2).

To indicate the meaning of liquidity and near moneyness more fully and their relationship to financial management and accounting detail, we may set forth some key accounts and indicate the order of the magnitudes of selected elements in the flows of returns per some common unit. To do this, let us recognize that a flow of returns from holding most assets consists of three elements—a yield (Q) or dollar flow of returns, less some carrying cost (C) or wastage over time, plus a liquidity element (L).[7] In the case of the liquidity element, there is nothing tangible to show for it, but, nevertheless, it represents a security and convenience associated with holding an asset. Thus, from the point of view of these elements and selected balance sheet accounts, there are inflows to be maximized for the

ALTERNATIVE SETS OF ASSETS	INFLOWS		OTHER ACCOUNTS	OUTFLOWS
	(A common dollar amount)			
	$Q - C$	L		L
Cash	O	+	Bank loans	–
Government securities and short-	↓	↑	Mortgages	↓
term investments	↓	↑	Bonds	↓
Instrumental capital (inventories	↓	↑	Capital stock	↓
and plant and equipment)	+	O		O

number of people working, and so on. Economic activity may be constant and still parallel an exponential growth in output and income (in constant prices) per annum; it may decline without output and income per annum declining; and it may increase with the result that the growth curve for output and income simply takes on a greater slope.

7. Keynes, *General Theory*, pp. 225-29; Frazer and Yohe, Sec. 4.1.

16

asset accounts and illiquidity or "immoneyness" to be minimized for accounts on the liabilities side as in the diagram.

On the one side, the dollar inflows $Q - C$) and liquidity (L) or "moneyness" are in the order of increasing returns and decreasing liquidity or moneyness, respectively. On the other side, the liquidity outflows are in the order of a decreasing liquidity drain or decreasing "immoneyness." This schematically presents the conflicting objectives as the basic conflict to be reconciled by managers.[8] Within the constraint imposed by the total of assets (and the corresponding total for liabilities and net worth) the management may increase risk and the flow of dollar returns at the expense of liquidity and vice versa. In terms of some combination of assets and claims against enterprises, the managers of business enterprise must find the level of liquidity that satisfies the transactions needs of firms and the managerial propensity (or aversion) to risk as well as that of the owners and bankers.

In terms of the above sketch, the numerator of the liquidity ratio includes assets with high liquidity and little or no yield, and the denominator includes liabilities such as bank loans with an increasing drain on liquidity. In decreasing the drain on liquidity from bank loans the ratio increases and in increasing liquidity from the flow of cash plus government securities it increases, and the reverse set of changes decreases the ratio. These two sets of changes together comprise the principal means of effecting liquidity adjustments, although these adjustments need not relate exclusively, or even primarily, to the use of (or the need for) temporary funds. The cash account, moreover, may be viewed as the account around which all other liquidity adjustments revolve and, in this narrower sense, we are in later chapters led to focus on an earlier (Sec. 1.1) measure of near moneyness.

Liquidity increases as funds are withdrawn from the capital market in the form of a sale of new stock and then used to increase liquid assets or reduce bank borrowing. It may increase also as funds flow in from increases in earned surplus and depreciation. In any event, the net flow of funds between firms and the financial markets may be *from* the financial markets, at times of rapid asset expansion, and there are times too when it may be *into* the financial markets.[9] The latter may occur when there are no new stock issues, or when repayment of bank loans and/or purchases of government and other liquid securities is, in part, made possible by the internal flow of funds from depreciation and retained earnings.

8. Robert W. Johnson, *Financial Management* (Boston: Allyn and Bacon, 1962), pp. 20 ff.

9. Frazer, "Large Manufacturing Corporations as Suppliers of Funds to the United States Government Securities Market," *Journal of Finance*, Dec., 1958, pp. 500-503.

2.3. SUMMARY

Income statements and balance sheets serve as sources of data. Retained earnings net of taxes, as shown on the income statement, are a source of corporate funds and the ratio of retained earnings to earnings net of taxes may serve as a means of measuring the relative importance of retained earnings for firms in different asset size groups. Any increase (decrease) in the accounts on the asset side of the balance sheets serves as a use (source) of funds, moreover; and any increase (decrease) in the accounts on the liabilities and net worth side serves as a source (use) of funds. In both instances, all sources and uses of funds revolve about the cash account, but the principal accounts reflecting the volition of financial managers and the capacity of enterprises to effect expenditures on short notice are those for cash, government or other liquid securities, and bank loans. The liquidity ratio contains these accounts and serves as a means of dealing with possible differences between the capacity of firms of different asset sizes to effect expenditures on short notice, in relation to asset size and independent of the dollar volume of assets in each asset size group.

The principal accounts reflecting the capacity of firms to obtain cash on short notice are government or similar liquid securities and bank loans. The ratio of these two accounts, consequently, serves as an indicator of near moneyness. It is also a means of dealing with the differences with respect to the near moneyness of varying asset size groups, again in relation to asset size and independent of the dollar volume of assets in each asset size group.

3. CHANGES IN THE FINANCIAL STRUCTURE OF FIRMS BY ASSET SIZE

This chapter deals with changes that occur in the financial structure of firms as they vary by asset size. The statistical results dealing with these changes are from analyses of cross section data. The changes are considered, first, in terms of the liquidity structure. In broad outline, overall changes in the financial structure are shown to reflect mainly the changes occurring in the liquidity structure. These changes are, in effect, differences in the financial structure of large vis-à-vis small firms, and they become important because of their relevance to contemporary monetary analysis. As pointed out elsewhere,[1] they are relevant to current monetary theory for several reasons.

(1) The main finding is that the larger sized firms have smaller cash balances, larger non-cash liquid asset holdings and less bank indebtedness, all relative to total

1. Frazer, "Financial Structure," p. 176.

assets, than smaller sized firms; (2) the latter set of changes reveals a decline in the demand for cash to satisfy the precautionary motive for holding cash, in relation to asset size, as firms increase in size; and (3) there is a tendency to overlook this latter variation in the strength of the precautionary motive in analyses of the demand for money.

The changes in question are revealed by the use of a statistical framework involving several particular characteristics as mentioned earlier (Sec. 1.2). One of these is the reliance upon linear approximations to relationships between sets of variables. The other concerns mid-points of class intervals for input values in the statistical analyses. Some may think the characteristics too simplifying, but for those I simply note several things: The results from linear approximations are interesting and useful in themselves; the present results are consistent with the implications of earlier analysis (Sec. 1.1); conclusions and analysis in subsequent chapters need not be thought of as relying upon the present results or conclusions; and what follows in subsequent chapters is consistent with the results of this chapter. For example, the results in this chapter are consistent with the notion whereby the turnover of money balances increases as a result of increases in liquidity (or index of near moneyness), yet the subsequent empirical confirmation of the truth of this notion (Table 5-3) is independent of the present analyses of data and the use of the mid-points of class intervals. The present use of linear approximations, of course, does not mean that additional and possibly even more satisfactory results will not come from a later work. Indeed, it is hoped that the present results and approach suggest future possibilities for other empirical studies.

3.1. THE PRECAUTIONARY MOTIVE AND CHANGES IN THE LIQUIDITY STRUCTURE

A definition of the precautionary demand of type 2 was set forth earlier and used in the proof of a principal proposition (Sec. 1.1). The proposition was that the precautionary demand of type 2 increases less than proportionally with wealth (or total assets), and presumably income with it. This we interpret to mean a number of things: that bank loans as a percentage of assets decline as firms increase in size, that this contributes to a decline in the precautionary demand for cash in relation to other assets, and that an overall result is a transfer of some cash as a percentage of assets to government securities. To provide empirical support for the proposition, therefore, we list statements of relationships and tests data concerning the statements. First, however, there is the stated assumption that income (or the dollar volume of sales) rises as wealth (or dollar value of assets) rises, and empirical support may also be given this assumption.

Income (*sales*) *and wealth* (*total assets*).—To provide empirical support for the assumption that income varies directly with wealth, a linear approximation was made to data. The data concerned the relationship between sales and total assets, and the data used were those reported for the 500 largest United States industrial corporations in 1962.[2] The result was as follows:

1.02 regression coefficient (b)

0.96 coefficient of determination (r^2)

As one may expect, the linear fit is nearly perfect. And the slope of the linear approximation is about 1; that is, an increase in assets corresponds to an increase in sales of about the same dollar amount. Assets (wealth) and sales (income) apparently vary directly.

Changes in the liquidity structure.—The following are statements pertaining to changes in the liquidity structure.

1. Corporate liquidity is directly related to asset size.
2. Government securities as a percentage of assets is directly related to asset size.
3. Cash as a percentage of assets is inversely related to asset size.
4. Total bank loans as a percentage of assets is inversely related to asset size.
5. Cash plus government securities as a percentage of assets is independent of asset size.

Statement 1 has no direct relationship to the above proposition but it does follow from the earlier definition of liquidity, statement 5, and statement 4, given little or no change in the ratio of current liabilities (other than bank loans) to total assets with respect to asset size. For example, in this context, the numerator of the liquidity ratio as a percentage of assets is relatively independent of asset size, and bank loans as a percentage of assets are a decreasing function of asset size. Apparently, given the ratio of current liabilities (other than bank loans) to total assets as being relatively independent of asset size, the liquidity ratio is an increasing function of asset size. The current liabilities other than bank loans include mainly "trade accounts and notes payable" and "federal income taxes accrued."

Table 3-1 contains the regression coefficients resulting from linear approximations to data concerning statements 1 to 5.[3] The coefficients are given in the table for each quarter, 1958-63, and there is a column of

2. See "Fortune Directory," 1963, pp. 177-96.

3. The data concerning statements 1 to 5 for years 1958-63 may be illustrated with reference to those for the 4th quarter, 1963 (accounts as percentages of total assets and the liquidity ratio as a percentage):

MID-POINT OF SIZE CLASS	LIQUIDITY RATIO	GOVERNMENT SECURITIES	CASH	BANK LOANS	CASH PLUS GOVERNMENT SECURITIES
0.5	.34	1.2	10.8	9.4	12.0
3.0	.38	2.2	8.9	9.2	11.2
7.5	.44	3.1	8.2	8.8	11.3
17.5	.48	3.5	7.6	8.3	11.2
37.5	.43	2.8	6.3	7.5	9.1
75.0	.50	3.2	6.6	5.1	9.8
175.0	.41	2.8	6.2	4.7	9.0
625.0	.35	2.3	4.8	3.5	7.1
1,500.0	.67	8.1	3.9	1.6	12.1

TABLE 3-1

REGRESSION COEFFICIENTS FOR RELATIONSHIPS AT END-OF-QUARTER DATES, 1958-63

Year and Quarter	Corporate Liquidity (as a percentage)[1] with Respect to Asset Size[4]	Government Securities[2] as Percentage of Assets with Respect to Asset Size	Cash as Percentage of Assets with Respect to Asset Size	Total Bank Loans[3] as a Percentage of Assets with Respect to Asset size	Cash Plus Government Securities as a Percentage of Assets with Respect to Asset Size
1958:					
1	.016*	.0028*	—.0029*	—.0040*	—.0001
2	.018*	.0029*	—.0032*	—.0042*	—.0003
3	.016*	.0028*	—.0037*	—.0041*	—.0009
4	.019*	.0037*	—.0037*	—.0039*	.0000
1959:					
1	.026*	.0043*	—.0031*	—.0042*	.0011
2	.027*	.0048*	—.0031*	—.0042*	.0017
3	.027*	.0044*	—.0033*	—.0044*	.0011
4	.024*	.0042*	—.0033*	—.0042*	.0009
1960:					
1	.022*	.0039*	—.0026*	—.0043*	.0013
2	.023*	.0039*	—.0027*	—.0044*	.0013
3	.019*	.0032*	—.0029*	— .0046*	.0003
4	.018*	.0034*	—.0031*	—.0044*	.0003
1961:					
1	.019*	.0030*	—.0028*	—.0044*	.0002
2	.023*	.0036*	—.0028*	—.0043*	.0007
3	.017*	.0028*	—.0031*	—.0044*	—.0004
4	.014*	.0031*	—.0034*	—.0040*	—.0003
1962:					
1	.013*	.0029*	—.0030*	—.0044*	—.0001
2	.015*	.0033*	—.0032*	—.0046*	.0002
3	.012*	.0025*	—.0031*	—.0048*	—.0006
4	.014*	.0033*	—.0033*	—.0044*	.0000
1963:					
1	.015*	.0033*	—.0030*	—.0047*	.0003
2	.016*	.0035*	—.0031*	—.0047*	.0004
3	.015*	.0031*	—.0032*	—.0050*	—.0002
4	.014*	.0033*	—.0031*	—.0047*	.0002

*Significantly different from zero at the 5 per cent level of significance.

1. Corporate liquidity = (cash + government securities/total current liabilities) × 100.

2. The category "government securities" is described by the data sources as including the "equivalent" of cash on hand; this would, presumably, include some non-cash marketable assets other than government securities.

3. Total bank borrowing includes short-term loans from banks (original maturity of one year or less), installments on long-term bank loans due in one year or less, and long-term bank loans due in more than one year.

4. There are nine classes of firms by asset size over the period in question. In millions of dollars these are: under 1, 1 to 5, 5 to 10, 10 to 25, 25 to 50, 50 to 100, 100 to 250, 250 to 1,000, and 1,000 and over.

Sources of data: U. S. Federal Trade Commission and Securities and Exchange Commission.

coefficients corresponding to each of the statements 1 to 5. The asterisks by the coefficients in the table indicate the results of tests of significance. They appear by those slope parameters that were shown to be significantly different from zero at the 5 per cent level of significance. One tail tests were made in the case of statements 1 to 4 and appropriate two tail tests were used in the instance where the dependent variable was viewed as being independent of asset size.

The results of the above tests, as shown in Table 3-1, provide strong evidence that statements 1 to 5 are true. The evidence, in turn, supports the principal proposition whereby the precautionary demand for money of type 2 declines relative to the demand for total assets as firms increase in size and as income increases. Within the above framework, moreover, these results imply that current liabilities other than bank loans—mainly accounts payable and accrued taxes as a percentage of assets—are only mildly or negatively related to asset size.[4]

Table 3-2 shows the coefficients of determination for the linear approximations to the data concerning statements 1 to 5. Apparently, from the information given in the table, relatively large proportions of the variations in the dependent variables in statements 1 to 4 are accounted for by the variation in asset size. By contrast, almost no variation in cash plus government securities as a percentage of assets appears to be accounted for by the variation in asset size. All of this is about as one would expect.

3.2. CHANGES IN THE FINANCIAL STRUCTURE: SOME FURTHER CONSIDERATIONS

Determining whether the changes in the financial structure of firms by asset size simply reflect changes in the liquidity structure requires further empirical evidence. Thus, to deal with the question, slope parameters, tests of data, and coefficients of determination concerning additional statements are reported. Comments relating to the question may be noted, for instance, about whether large firms are net lenders to small firms within the manufacturing sector through the extension of trade credit. The fact that sales finance affiliates of large firms are reported separately from the trade

4. Data for accounts payable and accrued taxes may be illustrated with reference to those for the 4th quarter, 1963 (accounts as percentages of total assets):

MID-POINT OF SIZE CLASS	TRADE ACCOUNTS AND NOTES PAYABLE	FEDERAL INCOME TAXES ACCRUED
0.5	18.4	3.0
3.0	12.6	3.7
7.5	9.3	3.8
17.5	7.7	3.6
37.5	7.1	3.5
75.0	6.4	3.8
175.0	7.4	3.7
625.0	7.2	3.5
1,500.0	7.5	4.6

credit extended by the manufacturing firms themselves may affect the results, but such comments have been made strictly with reference to the

TABLE 3-2

COEFFICIENTS OF DETERMINATION FOR LINEAR APPROXIMATIONS
AT END-OF-QUARTER DATES, 1958-63

Year and Quarter	Corporate Liquidity (as a percentage) with Respect to Asset Size	Government Securities as Percentage of Assets with Respect to Asset Size	Cash as Percentage of Assets with Respect to Asset Size	Total Bank Loans as a Percentage of Assets with Respect to Asset size	Cash Plus Government Securities as a Percentage of Assets with Respect to Asset Size
1958:					
1	.43	.68	.61	.93	.00
2	.44	.72	.69	.94	.01
3	.35	.68	.70	.93	.08
4	.39	.71	.70	.95	.00
1959:					
1	.54	.75	.72	.95	.12
2	.62	.82	.71	.88	.27
3	.62	.76	.69	.89	.13
4	.59	.75	.66	.92	.09
1960:					
1	.61	.76	.61	.93	.19
2	.65	.79	.64	.92	.21
3	.54	.72	.63	.92	.01
4	.47	.74	.64	.93	.01
1961:					
1	.49	.69	.59	.98	.01
2	.59	.75	.62	.91	.06
3	.48	.67	.61	.88	.02
4	.38	.70	.64	.86	.01
1962:					
1	.42	.64	.60	.86	.00
2	.49	.70	.60	.78	.00
3	.39	.59	.54	.75	.03
4	.47	.68	.55	.78	.00
1963:					
1	.48	.69	.58	.77	.01
2	.50	.70	.57	.73	.01
3	.51	.69	.57	.68	.00
4	.47	.71	.55	.70	.00

Sources of data: U. S. Federal Trade Commission and Securities and Exchange Commission.

FTC-SEC data for manufacturing firms[5] and, in any event, the affiliates would seem to deal primarily with the ultimate purchasers of durable goods and with wholesalers and retailers. In addition, changes in the financial structure of firms by asset size may reflect the extent of the re-

5. See Meltzer, "Mercantile Credit," pp. 429-36.

23

liance of the various asset size groups on retained earnings, long-term debt, and the use of equity funds other than retained earnings, all relative to asset size.

The role of trade credit.—With respect to receivables and payables, there is the possibility that the larger firms, even apart from sales finance affiliates, tend to extend larger amounts of trade credit in relation to that they use and in relation to their size than the smaller firms. If this were so, and if the differences between size groups were great, of course, the differences would show up in the ratio of accounts receivable to accounts payable in relation to asset size. To deal with the role of receivables and payables in the financial structure, therefore, the slope of linear approximations, tests of data, and coefficients of determination are reported below for the following statement.

6. The ratio of accounts receivable to accounts payable is independent of asset size.

Note that if the larger firms were on balance extending more trade credit to smaller firms within the manufacturing sector than they receive, then we would expect these developments to contribute to a rising ratio of accounts receivable to accounts payable with respect to asset size. Admittedly, there are other factors affecting the extension of trade credit, and here the question of whether large firms serve as net lenders to smaller firms within the corporate manufacturing sector is introduced in an overly simplified form. The question is only introduced in anticipation of a later topic (Chap. 6).

Retained earnings, long-term debt, owners' equity, and additional empirical evidence.—To deal with the possibility of major differences in financial structure resulting from variations in the reliance upon retained earnings, long-term debt, and sources of equity funds other than retained earnings, the slopes of linear approximations, tests of data, and coefficients of determination concerning the following additional statements are reported.

7. Retained earnings as a percentage of net profits are independent of asset size.
8. Long-term debt as a percentage of assets and exclusive of any long-term bank loans is independent of asset size.
9. Owner's equity as a percentage of assets is independent of asset size.

Table 3-3 contains the regression coefficients resulting from linear approximations to the data concerning statements 6 to 9.[6] As in Table 3-1, the coefficients are shown for the quarters 1958-63; there are columns of coefficients for statements 6 to 9; and asterisks denote slopes that are

6. The data concerning statements 6, 8, and 9 may be illustrated by those for the 4th quarter 1963 (accounts as percentages of total assets and the ratio of accounts receivable to accounts payable as a percentage):

significantly different from zero at the 5 per cent level of significance. The predominance of negative slopes for the ratio of accounts receivable to accounts payable reveal a decline in the ratio as asset size increases, but none of the slopes are significantly different from zero. Neither are any of the slopes for the columns corresponding to statements 8 and 9 significant, but the tendency for the slope parameters in the respective columns to have the same sign nevertheless means something. In fact, they reveal some relatively modest support for a decreasing functional relationship between the ratio of accounts receivable to accounts payable and asset size, and an increasing functional relationship for long-term debt as a percentage of asset size and asset size, respectively.

For ten of the twenty-four quarters, 1958-63, the slopes for retained earnings as a percentage of net profits are significant, and for nineteen of the twenty-four quarters they are negative.[7] These slopes would indicate that the larger firms are less inclined to rely on retained earnings in relation to asset size than the smaller firms. In terms of the tests reported in Table 3-3, the percentages are only mildly related to firms by asset size as contrasted with those in Table 3-1.

The coefficients of determination that concern statements 6 to 9 are set forth in Table 3-4. As one may note, these coefficients are small in relation to the ones shown earlier for statements 1 to 4. The coefficients of determination for the set of statements 6 to 9 tend to be the largest for retained earnings as a percentage of net profits with respect to asset size.

Changes in the liquidity and overall financial structures.—The percentages mentioned in statements 6 to 9 are only mildly related to asset size, and in view of the tests of significance, they are of less significance in relation to asset size than those mentioned in statements 1 to 4. The financial

MID-POINT OF CLASS SIZE	ACCOUNTS RECEIVABLE[1]	ACCOUNTS PAYABLE[2]	RATIO OF ACCOUNTS RECEIVABLE TO ACCOUNTS PAYABLE	LONG-TERM DEBT	OWNERS' EQUITY
0.5	26.8	18.4	1.45	11.8	50.6
3.0	22.8	12.6	1.81	8.3	59.4
7.5	21.6	9.3	2.32	8.5	62.7
17.5	19.5	7.7	2.53	9.5	64.2
37.5	19.2	7.1	2.71	11.3	63.8
75.0	16.9	6.4	2.63	11.5	65.6
175.0	16.0	7.4	2.15	13.4	61.5
625.0	13.7	7.2	1.89	15.5	61.0
1,500.0	11.4	7.5	1.52	9.1	69.8

[1]The FTC-SEC account in question is formally denoted "Other notes and accounts receivable (net)."
[2]The FTC-SEC account in question is formally denoted "Trade accounts and notes payable."
7. The coordinates of the observed points for retained earnings as a percentage of net profits with respect to asset size appear as follows for the 4th quarter, 1963.

MID-POINT OF SIZE CLASS	.5	3.0	7.5	17.5	37.5	75.0	175.0	625.0	1,500.0
RETAINED EARNINGS AS A PERCENTAGE OF NET PROFITS	.63	.63	.55	.54	.48	.46	.40	.49	.34

TABLE 3-3

REGRESSION COEFFICIENTS FOR RELATIONSHIPS AT
END-OF-QUARTER DATES, 1958-63

Year and Quarter	The Ratio (as a percentage) of Accounts Receivable to Accounts Payable[1] with Respect to Asset Size	Retained Earnings as a Percentage of Net Profits with Respect to Asset Size	Long-term Debt as a Percentage of Assets with Respect to Asset Size	Owners' Equity as a Percentage of Assets with Respect to Asset Size
1958:				
1..........	—.0513	.0292	.0019	.0034
2..........	—.0536	—.0296*	.0023	.0039
3..........	—.0594	—.0309*	.0027	.0037
4..........	—.0582	.0045	.0026	.0032
1959:				
1..........	—.0515	—.0111	.0024	.0037
2..........	—.0481	—.0163	.0022	.0039
3..........	—.0585	—.0372*	.0022	.0047
4..........	—.0509	—.0089*	.0018	.0045
1960:				
1..........	—.0488	—.0077	.0017	.0042
2..........	—.0550	—.0158	.0017	.0045
3..........	—.0562	—.0259*	.0016	.0048
4..........	—.0582	.0669	.0011	.0045
1961:				
1..........	—.0495	.0602*	.0010	.0050
2..........	—.0456	—.0169	.0012	.0053
3..........	—.0467	—.0267*	.0012	.0055
4..........	—.0472	—.0079	.0008	.0051
1962:				
1..........	—.0437	—.0067	.0007	.0050
2..........	—.0452	—.0196	.0008	.0055
3..........	—.0463	—.0265*	.0004	.0061
4..........	—.0489	—.0091	.0002	.0055
1963:				
1..........	—.0424	.0030	.0003	.0053
2..........	—.0407	—.0180*	.0004	.0055
3..........	—.0398	—.0200	.0003	.0064
4..........	—.0469	—.0132*	.0002	.0056

*Significantly different from zero at the 5 per cent level of significance.
1. The asset and liability accounts, respectively, are those reported by the data source as "other notes and accounts receivable (net)" and "other notes and accounts payable."
Sources of data: U. S. Federal Trade Commission and Securities and Exchange Commission.

structure of firms, consequently, must vary in relation to asset size mainly with respect to that portion of the structure involving the accounts for cash, government securities, and bank loans.

3.3. FIRMS' DEMANDS FOR LIQUIDITY: EARLIER IMPLICATIONS

The tendency for bank loans and for cash, both as percentages of assets,

TABLE 3-4

COEFFICIENTS OF DETERMINATION FOR LINEAR APPROXIMATIONS
AT END-OF-QUARTER DATES, 1958-63

Year and Quarter	The Ratio (as a percentage) of Accounts Receivable to Accounts Payable with Respect to Asset Size	Retained Earnings as a Percentage of Net Profits with Respect to Asset Size	Long-term Debt as a Percentage of Assets with Respect to Asset Size	Owners' Equity as a Percentage of Assets with Respect to Asset Size
1958:				
1.........	.26	.02	.08	.14
2.........	.27	.51	.10	.16
3.........	.32	.61	.14	.15
4.........	.38	.05	.13	.10
1959:				
1.........	.32	.26	.12	.13
2.........	.29	.41	.11	.14
3.........	.33	.77	.11	.22
4.........	.35	.30	.10	.19
1960:				
1.........	.26	.22	.11	.18
2.........	.27	.40	.10	.20
3.........	.26	.50	.11	.22
4.........	.35	.04	.06	.19
1961:				
1.........	.22	.45	.05	.22
2.........	.18	.37	.07	.23
3.........	.19	.50	.06	.25
4.........	.26	.19	.03	.22
1962:				
1.........	.23	.09	.02	.23
2.........	.20	.41	.02	.27
3.........	.22	.48	.01	.33
4.........	.33	.21	.00	.30
1963:				
1.........	.20	.01	.00	.25
2.........	.16	.46	.01	.28
3.........	.15	.42	.00	.34
4.........	.25	.48	.00	.28

Sources of data: U. S. Federal Trade Commission and Securities and Exchange Commission.

to decline in relation to increasing asset size serves as support for the proposition that the precautionary demand of type 2 for money balances does not increase proportionally with wealth (Sec. 1.1). The tendency for cash as a percentage of assets to be transferred to government security holdings, moreover, is consistent with an earlier view whereby holdings of government securities serve as a substitute for using bank credit as a means of reconciling temporary imbalances in the cash account. All of this—the tendency for the precautionary demand of type 2 to rise less than propor-

27

tionally with assets and the tendency for the money balances to be transferred to government securities—in combination with the relationship between sales and assets (Sec. 3.1), suggests other things. For one, it suggests that some substitute measure for the income velocity of money such as the ratio of sales to cash will vary directly with asset size. The latter relationship, then, in turn suggests that the amount of money balances demanded rises less than in proportion to the rise in income (and assets), and this prospect is in contrast to the view that the services rendered by money are a "luxury" (Sec. 1.2). The prospect and the contrast in views later lead to an examination of additional data (Chap. 7).

The above relationships and empirical results are consistent with, among other things, the view that liquidity as affected by a rising percentage of government securities and a declining percentage of bank borrowing is related to planned expenditures (Sec. 2.1). As an exercise in what determines firms' demands for liquidity, empirical findings have been shown to tentatively support the claim for such a relationship.[8] There is, in other words, some support for the view that liquidity is an indicator of future expenditures and that "among the less routine flows through cash are those involving financial planning for large capital expenditures" (Sec. 2.1).

Among the additional suggestions lurking behind the changes in the financial structure, as firms vary by asset size, is the one about the role of bank credit in conventional commercial loan doctrine (Sec. 4.1). There is, in particular, the suggestion that bank credit may not be a major source of funds for use in the acquisition of additional inventories, since bank loans as a percentage of assets decline as firms increase in size and since the comparable measure for inventories may not decline.

8. In the exercise, cross section data were analyzed concerning the following statement: "The indicator (i.e., corporate liquidity) for the planned level of desired money balances is directly related to the backlog of planned capital expenditures" (Frazer, "Financial Structure," p. 182). In the statistical analyses the X values were from the National Industrial Conference Board's survey of capital appropriations, the Y values were from corresponding industry classifications in the FTC-SEC *Quarterly Financial Report*, and the equation defining the approximations was $Y = bX + a$ (Sec. 1.2). Some explanation of the analyses is given in note 14 of my work cited above. The slope parameters resulting from the analyses and the results of t-tests for the quarters 1956 to 1961 are as follows.

1956:		1957:		1958:	
1	.024*	1	.023*	1	.027*
2	.026*	2	.026*	2	.029*
3	.025*	3	.023*	3	.033*
4	.023*	4	.023*	4	.030*
1959:		1960:		1961:	
1	.028*	1	.023*	1	.022*
2	.028*	2	.011	2	.029*
3	.044*	3	.025*	3	.021
4	.024*	4	.026*	4	.025*

*Significantly different from zero at the 5 per cent level of significance.

28

3.4. SUMMARY

The statistical findings indicate that bank loans and cash as percentages of assets decline as firms increase in size. These findings, in combination with that of a near-perfect direct relationship between income (sales) and wealth (assets), support the proposition that the precautionary demand for money rises less than proportionally with wealth or income (or sales). The results of linear approximations reveal, furthermore, a tendency for money balances as a percentage of assets to be transferred to securities and, given this tendency, the decline in bank loans contributes to a rise in liquidity in response to increasing asset size.

These findings are important for various reasons: Contemporary writers in the monetary area have been inclined to overlook certain aspects of the precautionary motive for holding money in their analyses and, somewhat along the same line, the findings indicate a need to examine certain prevailing views in contemporary monetary literature. There are other instances where a certain aspect of the precautionary motive, as defined earlier, has been overlooked, but one of these instances concerns the view that the services of money are a luxury. In contrast to this view, there is empirical support for the proposition that the precautionary demand rises less than proportionally with wealth (assets) and the relationship between wealth and income (or sales). This proposition and the relationship suggest that the ratio of sales to money balances must be rising, at least over some major portion of the domain over which asset sizes actually vary.

The pattern of changes in the accounts for bank loans and government securities lends empirical support to the possible significance of earlier suggestions that we thought were lurking behind the changes in the financial structure. In particular, in the next chapter we see whether the tendency for bank loans to decline foretells the presence of a relatively weak relationship between changes in inventories and the use of bank credit as a source of funds.

The results from linear approximations to data and tests concerning changes in the financial structure in relation to asset size indicate that the overall changes in the financial structure mainly reflect the changes in the liquidity structure. As opposed to the changes noted in the liquidity structure, linear approximations to relationships and tests of data suggest that the following are relatively independent of asset size: The ratio of accounts receivable to accounts payable, retained earnings as a percentage of net earnings, long-term debt as a percentage of assets, and owners' equity as a percentage of assets.

4. COMMERCIAL LOAN DOCTRINE
AND SOME EMPIRICAL FINDINGS

Early doctrine concerning commercial banks held that they should confine their loans to short-term commercial ones for, among other things, the purchase of inventories. The doctrine, moreover, had some impact on economic analysis. And this impact has caused some, even in modern times, to view changes in bank loans as a predominant source of funds for effecting changes in the short run in inventories. My own analysis and empirical findings,[1] on the other hand, have led me to an alternative view; namely, that as firms increase in size, they rely upon a varying mix of such alternative means of effecting adjustments in their cash accounts as the purchase and sale of government securities and the repayment and subsequent increase in bank loans. The logic of such an approach, according to me and others,[2] casts some doubt on the validity of the older view. As outlined below, it suggests structural differences in firms by asset size. In these differences the various classes may account for about the same percentages of assets in inventories while some size classes account for relatively small amounts of bank loans.[3] As Professor A. G. Hart has noted in response to such a comment about an earlier suggestion of his, "the possibilities of influencing inventories by moves toward the stabilization of business loans is manifestly much more remote than I suggested. . . ."[4]

Despite the latter positions, however, and whatever amount of sophistication about the matter may generally prevail, there is a scarcity of statistical analyses concerning the relationship between changes in bank loans and changes in inventories, and there has been no testing of data for the nine classes of manufacturing corporations by asset size as reported by the FTC-SEC since 1958. This chapter, therefore, does two things: It reviews credit doctrine concerning the relationship between changes in bank loans and changes in inventories, and presents some results from statistical analyses. The data analyzed are for the corporate manufacturing sector; the expenditures and financial behavior of this sector are of major importance[5]

---

1. See, e.g., Frazer, "Financial Structure," pp. 176-83.
2. Empirical findings reported by others would appear to be consistent with this approach; for a survey of previous findings and references to a study by Eisemann, in particular, see Paul F. McGouldrick, "The Impact of Credit Cost and Availability on Inventory Investment," *Inventory Fluctuations and Economic Stabilization* (*Part II*): *Causative Factors in Movements of Business Inventories* (Washington: U.S. G.P.O., 1962), pp. 99-106.
3. Frazer, "Financial Structure," p. 183.
4. "Making Monetary Policy More Effective," *United States Monetary Policy*, ed. Neil H. Jacoby (2d ed.; New York: Praeger, for the American Assembly, Columbia University, 1964), p. 234.
5. On the importance of this sector, see Bloch, "Short Cycles," pp. 1059-60.

as determinants of the behavior of aggregative measures of bank loans, inventories, output, and so on.

4.1. A REVIEW OF DOCTRINE

A tenet of commercial banking in the older days was that banks should confine their lending to short-term commercial loans.[6] There was the view that adherence to this rule would assure an adequacy of bank liquidity in the event of need for a contraction of loans, especially in response to an adverse balance of international payments and a loss of gold. As a practical matter, the doctrine was widely breached but, even so, there have been those who pointed to the presence of sounder banking conditions where it was observed.[7]

The doctrine had a great impact. It affected the writing of the original Federal Reserve Act, and the rules governing the operation of the System in its early years. Under those rules a Reserve bank was to take only "short-term self-liquidating agricultural, industrial, or commercial paper which was originally created for the purpose of providing funds for producing, purchasing, carrying or marketing of goods." As one prominent professor has noted, "according to this theory [referred to as the "needs of trade" theory] a bank could do no wrong so long as its loans were of the right *quality*—'sound' in the sense of being genuinely devoted to financing inventories (of finished goods, goods in process, or raw materials) on their way to sales."[8] Of course, in some ways the rule still lives on in the form of a broader emphasis on bank liquidity,[9] but—since the decline of the commercial loan business[10] relative to real estate, consumer loans, and so on—no one would still defend a strict adherence to the rule as a desirable guide for commercial or central banking practices. Referring to the Federal Reserve's resort to the use of voluntary credit restraint at

6. This rule or tenet has been variously referred to as the "commercial loan theory of banking" and the "real-bills doctrine." The former is traditionally American (see Lester V. Chandler, *The Economics of Money and Banking* [4th ed.; New York: Harper, 1964], pp. 202-3), but of course the rule is not a theory in the sense of a formal model (or explanation of real phenomena) with assumptions and conclusions that can be accepted (or rejected) by references to empirical facts and tests of data. The latter term is English; see Hart, *Money Debt and Economic Activity*, (2d ed.; New York, Prentice-Hall, 1953), pp. 56-57; Lloyd W. Mintz, *History of Banking Theory* (University of Chicago Press, 1945), p. 18 *et passim*.

7. Paul B. Trescott, *Financing American Enterprise: A Story of Commercial Banking* (New York: Harper, 1963), pp. 23-24, 35-36.

8. Hart, "Making Monetary Policy More Effective."

9. See Chandler, *Money and Banking*, pp. 202-3; Chandler, *Benjamin Strong, Central Banker* (Washington: Brookings Institution, 1958), pp. 194-95.

10. For a work along these lines see Neil H. Jacoby and Raymond J. Saulnier, *Business Financing and Banking* (National Bureau of Economic Research, 1947); see also Trescott, pp. 188-89, 173.

commercial banks during the Korean War inflation, however, Hart notes that "the emphasis on financing production in the 'voluntary restraint' guide-lines (including validation of loans to permit financing inventory at higher prices) harked back to the needs of trade theory. . . ."[11]

The doctrine also had some impact on economic analysis. It caused some to look to the control over the use of credit for carrying business inventories as a means of achieving a greater stability in business expenditures (or an "equilibrium between the production of goods and their consumption").[12] This was true even with respect to some who would deny the appropriateness of the doctrine as a guide for the conduct of monetary policy. One finds, for example, even in modern times, the implication that apparent parallel movements in time series for bank loans and business inventories reflect a use of bank loans as a means of carrying inventories.[13] However, it should be noted that the analyst, in the latter instance, has more recently recognized the greater remoteness of the relationship between bank loans and inventory purchases. Writing in the second edition of *United States Monetary Policy*, Hart makes the following statement.

> In the first edition of this volume, I instanced the interesting relation between the time-shape of business loans of commercial banks and that of business inventories. Mr. William Frazer points out that a large fraction of the inventory is in lines of manufacturing where loans are relatively trifling. There is still an interesting relation if we subtract out most branches of manufacturing both from inventories and from business loans; but the possibilities of influencing inventory by moves toward stabilization of business loans is manifestly much more remote than I suggested in the first edition.[14]

4.2. SOME EMPIRICAL FINDINGS

To deal with some questions about the financial structure of firms and the use of bank loans we now do several things: Review some series from the *Quarterly Financial Report* (Sec. 1.2) for end-of-quarter totals for bank loans and inventories and for first differences in the totals, report on the results of some analyses of cross section data for firms by asset size, and report on the results of some analyses of time series data for firms by asset size. The results from the analyses of cross section data deal with the question of whether structural differences in firms by asset size affect the relationship between bank loans and inventories. The results from the analyses of time series data deal with questions about the rela-

11. "Making Monetary Policy More Effective."
12. See Milton Friedman and Anna Jacobson Schwartz, *A Monetary History of the United States, 1867-1960* (Princeton University Press for the National Bureau of Economic Research, 1963), pp. 252-53.
13. See Hart, "Making Monetary Policy Effective," *loc. cit.*, 1st ed., 1958, pp. 186-87.
14. See Hart, "Making Monetary Policy More Effective," p. 234.

tionships between bank loans as a source of funds and expenditures on inventories.

Quarterly totals, first differences, and results from the analyses of cross

TABLE 4-1

BANK LOANS AND INVENTORIES FOR
MANUFACTURING CORPORATIONS:
TIME SERIES FOR TOTAL AMOUNTS AND
FIRST DIFFERENCES, 1959-1963

(Dollar amounts in millions)

| Year and Quarter | TOTAL AMOUNTS[1] | | FIRST DIFFERENCES[2] | |
	Bank Loans	Inventories	Δ Bank Loans	Δ Inventories
1959:				
1	11,365	54,592	735	1,593
2	11,407	55,756	42	1,164
3	11,662	55,796	215	40
4	11,695	57,875	33	2,079
1960:				
1	13,041	60,157	1,346	2,282
2	13,653	60,530	612	373
3	13,805	60,491	152	—39 [3]
4	13,393	60,360	—412	—131
1961:				
1	14,196	61,298	803	938
2	13,987	60,855	—987	—443
3	13,712	61,124	—275	269
4	13,394	62,800	—318	1,676
1962:				
1	13,657	64,520	263	1,720
2	13,701	65,195	44	675
3	14,217	65,677	516	482
4	14,059	66,621	—158	944
1963:				
1	14,522	68,028	463	1,407
2	14,301	68,705	—221	677
3	14,773	69,136	472	431
4	14,136	70,539	—637	1,403

1. Total amounts such as stocks of inventories are at end of quarter dates.
2. The first differences are changes during the respective quarters.
3. The encircled pairs of quarter-to-quarter changes in bank loans and inventories represent instances where the respective changes have different signs.
The FTC-SEC data are not entirely satisfactory for absolute measures for selected accounts (see comments in Sec. 1.2.).
Sources of data: U. S. Federal Trade Commission and Securities and Exchange Commission.

section data.—The end-of-quarter totals for bank loans and inventories and the first differences in these totals, for the years 1958-63, are shown in Table 4-1. Even in this table of data for only the corporate manufacturing sector, one may note some tendency for the total amounts for bank loans and inventories to move in the same direction. There one notes that quarter-to-quarter changes move in the same direction about 70 per cent of the time and the opposite direction the remainder of the time. Those instances where the changes move in the opposite direction are encircled.

However, we are presently more interested in time series changes in bank loans with respect to those in inventories for firms by asset size. This is because a relatively weak relationship between the latter sets of changes was loosely suggested by structural matters concerning the tendency for bank loans (as a percentage of assets) to decline as size increases. The tendency seemed to suggest that larger firms carried smaller percentages of assets in inventories or that the ratio of bank loans to inventories declined as asset size increased. Thus, before proceeding with the results from analyses of time series data, cross section data are analyzed concerning the following statement.

The ratio of total bank loans to inventories is a decreasing function of asset size.[15]

The results of analyses of data for the latter relationship are shown in Table 4-2. As one would expect, the slope parameters are all negative, the coefficients of determination are reasonably large, and the negative slopes are all significantly different from zero. Apparently, it is reasonable to conclude that the firms relying most heavily on bank loans in relation to asset size may not be carrying comparably larger percentages of assets in inventories in relation to other firms, and, conversely, the firms relying least heavily on bank loans in relation to asset size may not be carrying comparably smaller percentages of assets in inventories in relation to other firms.

This is very interesting, but it is simply a basis for the speculation that time series changes in inventories for manufacturing corporations by asset size are not strongly related to time series changes in bank loans for such firms by asset size. We now turn to the results from the analyses of time series data for firms by asset size.

15. The data for bank loans and inventories for firms by asset size may be illustrated with reference to those for the 4th quarter 1963:

MID-POINT OF SIZE CLASS	BANK LOANS AS A PERCENTAGE OF ASSETS	INVENTORIES (BOOK VALUE) AS A PERCENTAGE OF ASSETS	THE RATIO (AS A PERCENTAGE) OF BANK LOANS TO INVENTORIES
.5	9.4	25.0	.38
3.0	9.2	29.5	.31
7.5	8.8	28.9	.31
17.5	8.3	28.7	.28
37.5	7.5	28.5	.26
75.0	5.1	26.1	.19
175.0	4.7	27.1	.17
625.0	3.5	26.2	.13
1,500.0	1.6	15.1	.12

Some results from the analyses of time series data.—There may be some interesting relations between "the time-shape of business loans of commercial banks and that of business inventories." Further, some of these relationships may appear less interesting when the series are disaggregated, but the major question with which we are presently concerned is more simply this: Do time series data from financial statements (Chap. 2) for manufacturing corporations by asset size reveal strong and relatively direct relationships between the use of funds from bank loans and the purchase of inventories? Also, we may ask whether there are any significant rela-

TABLE 4-2

THE RATIO (AS A PERCENTAGE) OF TOTAL BANK LOANS TO
INVENTORIES WITH RESPECT TO ASSET SIZE:
RESULTS FROM CROSS SECTION DATA, 1958 TO 1963

Year and Quarter	COEFFICIENTS		Year and Quarter	COEFFICIENTS	
	Regression (b)	Determination (r^2)		Regression (b)	Determination (r^2)
1958:			1961:		
1	—.0156*	.32	1	—.0120*	.90
2	—.0114*	.90	2	—.0112*	.77
3	—.0124*	.88	3	—.0131*	.77
4	—.0112*	.84	4	—.0110*	.71
1959:			1962:		
1	—.0123*	.90	1	—.0125*	.73
2	—.0120*	.85	2	—.0133*	.67
3	—.0131*	.86	3	—.0146*	.67
4	—.0117*	.90	4	—.0127*	.62
1960:			1963:		
1	—.0119*	.93	1	—.0132*	.61
2	—.0120*	.92	2	—.0133*	.58
3	—.0132*	.91	3	—.0143*	.60
4	—.0120*	.87	4	—.0133*	.56

*Significantly different from zero at the 5 per cent level of significance.
Sources of data: U. S. Federal Trade Commission and Securities and Exchange Commission.

tionships between the use of funds from bank loans and the purchase of inventories, as revealed by analyses of data for firms by asset size. It would seem that a disaggregation of data, comparable to that revealing the differences in the financial structure of firms, would be most helpful in answering the questions. This would seem true because in such disaggregation of data we avoid some of the interference from the structural matters outlined above.

To deal with these questions, linear approximations were made to the data for nine asset size classes comprising the corporate manufacturing sector. These were made as a means of getting several sets of empirical results: (1) slope parameters for the relationships between bank loans and inventories for the different asset size groups, (2) tests of the signifi-

35

cance of differences between the empirical slopes and some theoretical slopes, and (3) coefficients of determination. The data tested pertain to the following statement.[16]

> The dollar amount of bank loans (as indicated by quarterly changes in short-term and both short- and long-term bank loans) is an increasing function of expenditures on inventories (as indicated by quarterly changes in the book value of inventories).

The empirical slopes concerning the latter statement were tested for their significant difference from one and zero respectively. The theoretical slope of one was used, in the first instance, because one is the slope expected, if changes in inventories are entirely financed from bank loans and if bank loans to manufacturing corporations are strictly inventory loans. Admittedly, the latter hypothesis is likely to be false. But if there is the suggestion in monetary literature and discussions that time series for bank loans and inventories move parallel to one another (as when the slopes of tangents to the two series are equal at any given time), then the hypothesis concerning the slope of one is implicit in the suggestion. I believe there has been sufficient evidence (e.g., note 13) to warrant the testing of this strong hypothesis.

The theoretical slope of zero was used, in the second instance above, simply as a means of dealing with the statement about some increasing functional relationship. Quite likely some portion of changes in inventories is at least occasionally financed by bank loans as the overall thesis of this essay implies.

Table 4-3 summarizes the results pertaining to the relationship between changes in short-term bank loans and changes in inventories (book value). In Column (1) of the table we note that the slopes of the regression lines are significantly different from one. This, then, leads to a rejection of the strong hypothesis that is suggested by references to possible parallel

---

16. We are not presently concerned with the questions of the effects of the cost and availability of bank credit on the decisions to purchase inventories; see on these William H. White, *Inventory Investment and the Rate of Interest*, Reprint No. 57 (Washington: Brookings Institution, 1962), reprinted from *Banca Nazionale del Lavoro Quarterly Review*, June, 1961. We have avoided these questions because our approach would indicate that such questions should more readily arise in connection with the broader study of cyclical changes in the demand for money, other assets, and the entire range of the alternative means of financing. In this narrower sense, then, as one Federal Reserve economist says, "the relevant comparison in studying inventory investment . . . is between changes in inventories and changes in bank loans. Since such inventory working capital is a permanent component of total capital, it is not surprising that this component should be financed, like fixed capital, from stockholders' investment, retained earnings, and long-term nonbank borrowing. However, this permanent component is irrelevant for decisions at the margin of investment." (McGouldrick, "Impact of Credit Cost," p. 94.)

movements in the series for bank loans and inventories, at least with respect to short-term loans.

The results of the tests reported in Column (2) of Table 4-3, on the other hand, provide some support for the above statement concerning the presence of some increasing functional relationship. The slope parameters are all positive, but they are, in addition, significantly different from zero for four of the nine asset size groups—namely, 10 to 25, 25 to 50, 50 to 100, and 250 to 1,000 million dollars. As the coefficients of determination in Column (3) indicate, the portion of the changes in short-term

TABLE 4-3

QUARTERLY CHANGES IN SHORT-TERM BANK LOANS WITH RESPECT
TO CHANGES IN INVENTORIES (BOOK VALUE):
RESULTS FROM TIME SERIES DATA, 2D QUARTER
1958 TO 3D QUARTER 1963

| Firms by Asset Size (dollar amounts in millions) | REGRESSION COEFFICIENTS (b's) | | Coefficients of Determination (r^2's) Col. (3) |
	Tested for Significant Difference from One Col. (1)	Tested for Significant Difference from Zero Col. (2)	
Under 1	0.07*	0.07	0.03
1 to 5	0.08*	0.08	0.02
5 to 10	0.18*	0.18	0.09
10 to 25	0.24*	0.24†	0.17
25 to 50	0.25*	0.25†	0.20
50 to 100	0.31*	0.31†	0.33
100 to 250	0.09*	0.09	0.06
250 to 1,000	0.17*	0.17†	0.16
Over 1,000	0.03*	0.03	0.11

*Significantly different from one at the 5 per cent level of significance, using the two-tail test and allowing for 20 degrees of freedom.
†Significantly different from zero at the 5 per cent level, using the one-tail test, and allowing for 20 degrees of freedom.
Sources of data: U. S. Federal Trade Commission and Securities and Exchange Commission.

loans that is accounted for by changes in inventories varies over a range from about 2 per cent for firms in the 1 to 5 million asset-size group to about 33 per cent for the 50 to 100 group.

These latter results are about what we would expect. Funds for the purchase of inventories come from a variety of sources. Short-term bank loans are apparently only one of the sources, relative to the total of funds used in the short run.

Table 4-4 summarizes the results for the relationship between changes in short- plus long-term bank loans and inventories. The results reported there support about the same conclusions as those drawn above. The slope parameters in Table 4-4, however, increase for eight of the nine classes, and more of the variation in bank loans appears to be accounted for by the variation in inventories when both short- and long-term bank loans are considered together.

A comparison of the information in Tables 4-3 and 4-4 suggests the use of some long-term borrowing to finance inventories. This need not mean that the purpose given for the borrowing will be to finance inventories, for the borrowed funds may go for other purposes and simply release other funds for inventory purchases.

Apparently, in view of the results from analyses of data and in answer

TABLE 4-4

QUARTERLY CHANGES IN BANK LOANS (SHORT- PLUS LONG-TERM)
WITH RESPECT TO CHANGES IN INVENTORIES (BOOK VALUE):
RESULTS FROM TIMES SERIES DATA 2D QUARTER
1958 TO 3D QUARTER 1963

| Firms by Asset Size (dollar amounts in millions) | REGRESSION COEFFICIENTS (b's) | | |
	Tested for Significant Difference from One (Col. (1)	Tested for Significant Difference from Zero Col. (2)	Coefficients of Determination (r^2's) (Col. (3)
Under 1	.14*	0.14	0.08
1 to 5	0.16*	0.16	0.06
5 to 10	0.21*	0.21	0.11
10 to 25	0.25*	0.25†	0.18
25 to 50	0.33*	0.33†	0.21
50 to 100	0.37*	0.37†	0.18
100 to 250	0.11*	0.11	0.07
250 to 1,000	0.17*	0.17†	0.16
Over 1,000	0.07*	0.07	0.13

*Significantly different from one at the 5 per cent level of significance, using the two-tail test and allowing for 20 degrees of freedom.
†Significantly different from zero at the 5 per cent level, using the one-tail test, and allowing for 20 degrees of freedom.
Sources of data: U. S. Federal Trade Commission and Securities and Exchange Commission.

to the major question, there are no strong and relatively direct relationships between the use of funds from bank loans and the purchase of inventories for manufacturing corporations. But, as we would expect and, as the overall approach of this essay implies, some portion of changes in inventories is at least occasionally financed by bank loans.

4.3. SUMMARY

The commercial loan doctrine about bank credit held, among other things, that commercial banks should confine their lending activities to short-term, self-liquidating, commercial loans. This doctrine had its impact on the writing of the original Federal Reserve Act, on the early operations of some Fereral Reserve banks, and on economic analysis. In the latter case, it led to the view that apparent parallel movements in bank loans and inventories reflected a use of bank loans as a means of financing inventories. As matters have evolved, the Federal Reserve Act has changed, and no economist or operating banker would expect a commercial bank to adhere to the stringent rules of the early doctrine. There are, nevertheless, references in modern times to changes in business loans by banks as a predominant source of funds for the purchase of inventories in the short run, and in any event, there has been a scarcity of satisfactory tests of data concerning the relationship between changes in bank loans and inventory changes.

In fact, there is a structural factor—the decreasing ratio of bank loans to inventories with respect to asset size—which suggests some imperfection and irregularity in the relationships between bank loans as a source of funds and the purchase of inventories. Some asset size groups use more bank funds in relation to inventories than others.

To deal more thoroughly with the latter relationships, the relevant data for nine classes of manufacturing corporations were analyzed. The results show that changes in bank loans to manufacturing firms are an increasing function of changes in inventories; but the slopes for the linear approximations to the data for the different asset size classes are significantly different from zero for less than half of the asset size classes.

What may appear as parallel movements in series for some aggregates for bank loans to manufacturing firms and inventories should not be interpreted as a use of such loans for financing short-run increases in inventories. Some portion of funds from both short- and long-term bank loans may be used to purchase inventories, but the experience of different asset size groups is quite diverse. For a given increase in inventories, some asset size classes will use bank loans as a source of financing to more than twice the extent of other classes by asset size, as indicated by the respective slopes of our linear approximations.

5. THE DEMAND FOR MONEY, GOVERN-MENT SECURITIES, AND BANK LOANS: SOME CRITICAL AND OTHER COMMENTS

There are some elements of inconsistency in the approaches or conclusions of some 1963-64 articles and the present approach or results from analyses of data. In one of the articles Professor Ernest Bloch,[1] among other things, placed strong emphasis on the role of a category called "tax" governments as a special account for effecting adjustments in

1. "Short Cycles."

firms' tax liabilities, and he fails to recognize explicitly the role of decreases in the indebtedness of business firms at the bank as a substitute for government security holdings or as a source of liquidity or moneyness. In another, Professor Richard H. Timberlake, Jr.,[2] among other things, wrote of "immoneyness" or bank indebtedness as a neglected factor affecting the demand for money. He also outlined some criticisms of certain aspects of the emphasis in monetary theory on a relationship between turnover of money balances and money substitutes. The earlier chapters of this essay, on the other hand, have placed emphasis on "immoneyness" or "illiquidity" (Secs. 1.1, 2.2, and 3.3) in the form of firms' indebtednesses at the bank as well as upon the role of government security holdings. This chapter, therefore, contains an outline of some of the conflicting conclusions concerning certain aspects of the demand for money and so-called money substitutes as these pertain to the corporate manufacturing sector.

Additional empirical findings are also presented in this chapter. They pertain to the divergent points of view and to some theoretical matters. The findings are consistent with the approach set forth in the previous chapters of this essay, and they are presented as support for that rather general approach in contrast to others. In previous chapters all transactions have been viewed as revolving about the cash account (Sec. 2.1), the principal accounts for effecting adjustments in cash have been viewed as government securities and bank loans (Sec. 2.2), and an introductory question (Sec. 1.1) anticipated a relationship between the turnover of money balances and the index of near moneyness. In these chapters, then, money substitutes make a difference and, in addition, any large cash payment, such as the payment of corporate income taxes, is highly likely to temporarily involve corporate liquidity generally and to be met by an increase in indebtedness at the bank, a decrease in corporate holdings of government securities, or by a reduction in surplus cash. The present approach, consequently, would appear to be in conflict with an approach that emphasizes a special pool of liquid assets (namely, "tax" governments) for effecting adjustments in a specific liability (namely, accrued federal taxes). It would also be somewhat inconsistent with conclusions that denied the presence of a relationship between the turnover of money balances and so-called money substitutes.

5.1. "Tax" Governments, "Free" Governments, and the Demand for Government Securities and Money

Professor Bloch, in his *American Economic Review* article, assumes distinct categories for the government security holdings of manufacturing

2. "Stock of Money."

corporations. These include "tax" governments and "free" governments, where *"tax" governments + "free" governments = total governments* (i.e., holdings of government securities by asset size classes, or by the firm, depending on the context of the analysis), *"tax" governments = tax liabilities*, and *"free" governments = total governments – tax liabilities*. In the form of the "specific hypothesis," Bloch claims that "free governments serve as a financial reserve pool for *unknown* future investment outlays" (italics added).

In dealing with these matters, in this section, we do several things. We review the evidence for the assumption underlying Bloch's approach, review reasoning leading to such an approach, and present results of statistical tests as they would apparently follow from that approach. We also review some earlier results bearing directly on Bloch's "specific hypothesis." In attempting to show that "free" governments lack the uniqueness attributed to them by Bloch, we note that he neglected the role of decreases in the indebtedness of firms at the bank as a part of the "financial reserve pool" and, in so doing, we anticipate Timberlake's emphasis on a "neglected" factor (namely, the "immoneyness" or indebtedness at the bank). The review of the evidence supporting the use of the two categories for government securities has a significance extending beyond Bloch's use of them. Others, as noted by Bloch,[3] have used the term "free" governments.

"Tax" governments, "free" governments, and some statistical findings.—A key variable in Professor Bloch's discussion of the corporate demand for government securities and money is that for "free" governments—i.e., "total governments less tax liabilities." He emphasizes this variable throughout his *American Economic Review* article, and notes that the government securities in question "serve as a kind of 'secondary liquidity reserve' for the large manufacturing corporations" (i.e., those with over 100 million dollars in assets). He treats these as a distinct "pool" to be used to effect cash adjustments, although he also points out (p. 1063) that "the actual assets held" for discharging tax liabilities and for unknown future capital expenditures "could be the same credit instruments (say, Treasury bills)."

Bloch assumes (p. 1062) that "holdings of 'free governments' should be kept conceptually and functionally distinct from the holdings of 'tax governments' or other types of liquid assets held for similar payments. . . ." The rationale for the assumptions is apparently set forth in several statements (pp. 1060-62).

(1) "The smaller corporations [100 million dollars and less] managed to boost their holdings of governments to parity with tax liabilties by 1959. . . ."

3. "Short Cycles," note 7.

(2) "Throughout the period a near perfect intra-year coordination of changes in tax liabilities and of government holdings of the smaller corporations also impart to their holdings of governments a substantial degree of seasonality."

(3) "For large corporations [100 million dollars and over], on the other hand, the direction of changes of holdings of governments and of tax liabilities is not always the same."

Having made these statements, Bloch then proceeds to analyze the behavior of "free" governments as if he has accounted for the behavior of "tax" governments. His empirical support for the use of "tax" governments as a distinct stock of securities is a sketch of the intra-year coordination of changes in tax liabilities and of government holdings of the smaller corporations. Bloch's statements, his approach, and his sketch, nevertheless, seem to suggest a much stronger notion than simply that of a relationship between changes in tax liabilities and changes in cash, indebtedness at the bank, or the stock of government securities held by manufacturing corporations. They seem, in contrast, to suggest that a reduction in tax liabilities is carried out with funds from a reduction in so-called "tax" governments and that an increase in the liabilities calls forth an approximately equal increase in "tax" governments, all on a quarter by quarter basis, for firms with assets under 100 million dollars. Note that according to Bloch's dichotomy, the only government securities held by corporations with assets below 100 million dollars are "tax" governments.

A simple break down of the aggregates for quarterly changes in "tax" governments and tax liabilities, however, does not provide support for the stronger notion in question. Table 5-1, where the ordered pairs of changes are shown for the classes of firms with assets under 100 million dollars, indicates instead that over one-third of the changes comprising the ordered pairs fail to have the same sign. Such instances are indicated by the encircled pairs in the table. It may be noted, too, that in the instances of a common sign for the corresponding changes in government securities and tax liabilities, the magnitudes of the changes in one variable are not too likely to be predictive of the magnitudes of the changes in the corresponding variable.

Bloch's basis for the netting out of "tax" governments and his proceeding to explain only "free" governments suggest a slope of one (i.e., $b = 1.00$) and a coefficient of determination of one (i.e., $r^2 = 1.00$), for the relationship between changes in government security holdings and changes in tax liabilities for classes of firms with assets below 100 million dollars. Otherwise Bloch arbitrarily leaves out large batches of some unexplained government securities as he proceeds with his analysis. Thus, to deal further with Professor Bloch's basic assumption, tests of data concerning the above slope of one were made. The results of these tests and the coefficients of determination are shown in Table 5-2 for six classes of

TABLE 5-1

FOR FIRMS WITH ASSETS BELOW 100 MILLION DOLLARS, 1959-63
QUARTERLY CHANGES IN GOVERNMENT SECURITIES AND TAX LIABILITIES

(Dollar amounts in millions)

Year and Quarter	Under 1 Δ Government Securities	Under 1 Δ Tax Liabilities	1 to 5 Δ Government Securities	1 to 5 Δ Tax Liabilities	5 to 10 Δ Government Securities	5 to 10 Δ Tax Liabilities	10 to 25 Δ Government Securities	10 to 25 Δ Tax Liabilities	25 to 50 Δ Government Securities	25 to 50 Δ Tax Liabilities	50 to 100 Δ Government Securities	50 to 100 Δ Tax Liabilities
1959:												
1	− 5	− 66	− 24	− 26	− 7	− 48	21	− 32	− 4	− 29	−107	− 68
2	− 6	65	− 20	14	− 28	− 17	− 22	− 35	8	− 29	− 48	− 67
3	11	82	64	124	14	60	90	83	82	60	157	105
4	50	10	56	21	43	6	40	28	7	38	58	40
1960:												
1	11	−113	− 1	−140	− 39	− 86	−139	−144	− 80	− 56	− 86	−107
2	− 17	− 8	− 92	− 67	− 33	− 17	− 73	− 45	− 87	− 42	− 63	− 58
3	− 11	84	− 10	58	0	− 27	14	26	− 4	− 17	26	18
4	− 3	− 26	41	− 7	30	− 16	23	− 22	11	− 23	− 7	4
1961:												
1	15	−104	− 66	−126	− 12	− 61	− 63	−104	− 6	− 99	−103	− 66
2	− 44	15	− 34	13	− 44	8	− 41	8	− 40	9	− 38	21
3	− 1	81	− 2	135	16	46	15	58	37	40	32	62
4	13	48	19	76	17	33	4	41	53	46	13	59
1962:												
1	3	− 91	25	− 92	− 42	− 34	− 3	− 42	− 53	− 20	− 63	−107
2	− 10	52	− 34	23	− 14	− 15	− 52	12	− 41	− 14	− 32	34
3	7	90	29	118	48	39	28	53	39	40	5	67
4	− 18	− 8	− 25	− 9	13	21	23	4	35	8	9	− 18
1963:												
1	− 31	− 98	30	− 48	− 29	− 40	− 24	− 81	− 79	− 65	− 51	− 86
2	23	52	− 72	− 8	− 15	− 10	− 12	− 14	− 16	− 7	− 31	0
3	16	115	28	85	− 12	− 26	28	60	6	60	49	74
4	− 4	0	18	45	44	23	15	12	52	22	89	27

Note: The encircled pairs indicate instances in which ordered pairs of changes in government security holdings and accrued federal income taxes fail to have the same sign.

Sources of data: U. S. Federal Trade Commission and Securities and Exchange Commission.

firms with assets under 100 million dollars. The table presents evidence from time series.

The results summarized in Table 5-2 indicate that there is no strong relationship of the type implied by Bloch's approach. The regression coefficients increase up to 50 million dollars and then they drop somewhat for the last class. The coefficients of determination, moreover, indicate that only 6 per cent of the changes in government security holdings can be accounted for by changes in tax liabilities for the smallest size class. They also indicate that the extent of the changes accounted for increases up to no more than 56 per cent in the case of the 50 to 100 million dollar asset size class. These latter coefficients of determination, of

TABLE 5-2

QUARTERLY CHANGES IN GOVERNMENT SECURITIES WITH RESPECT
TO CHANGES IN TAX LIABILITIES:
EVIDENCE FROM TIMES SERIES DATA

| Asset Size Class (in millions of dollars) | COEFFICIENTS | |
	Regression (b)	Determination (r^2)
Under 1	0.13*	0.06
1 to 5	0.21*	0.17
5 to 10	0.46*	0.30
10 to 25	0.54*	0.46
25 to 50	0.77	0.52
50 to 100	0.68*	0.56

*The slope parameter b is significantly different from one at the five per cent level of significance, with the appropriate 2-tail tests.
1. The period covered is 1st-quarter 1958 to 3rd-quarter 1963. There are 22 quarters covered for each asset-size class, and, consequently, 20 degrees of freedom for each.
2. There are six asset size classes reported in the FTC-SEC sample of manufacturing corporations with assets under 100 million dollars over the period since 1958.
Sources of data: U. S. Federal Trade Commission and Securities and Exchange Commission.

course, offer some support for the use of governments as a source of funds for making tax payments and, indeed, most large outlays will likely be effected by a reduction in government security holdings and cash, and/or an increase in bank loans. The assumption on which Professor Bloch proceeds, however, is a much stronger one, and the results in Table 5-2 do not support the assumption as outlined above.

An accounting identity and the "specific hypothesis."—Now, we attempt to illustrate two things: That Professor Bloch's statistical analysis is carried out within the framework of an accounting identity, and that, in contrast to his view, his "specific hypothesis" could have been stated for bank loans as well as for government securities. Bloch says (p. 1065),

We will attempt to show . . . that when major corporate uses of funds (i.e., total spending on net inventories and on plant and equipment) exceed major sources of funds (i.e., both internal and outside funds), free governments will be sold.

44

The converse is also said to hold and the "major sources are said to include bank loans, funds from capital market flotations, and funds from retained earnings and depreciation reserves." In the latter framework, a *deficit* is an excess of corporate uses, and a *surplus* is an excess of funds from major sources, including bank loans. The residual categories, in this framework, are cash, net trade credit, "free" governments, other governments (tax liabilities, by definition), and tax liabilities. But, in view of the definitional equality of the latter two categories, the residuals are reduced to three: cash, net trade credit, and "free" governments.

Any deficit, as defined above, must be met from a net reduction in some combination of the latter categories, and a surplus results in some net accumulation. Even so, the only category of any consequence that is left to vary in response to a deficit or a surplus is "free" governments, in view of the likely quarter-to-quarter variation in net trade credit (Sec. 2.1, and Chap. 6), and in view of routine experience concerning the management of cash in such a tautological framework.[4]

Surpluses (or deficits) accounting for a large percentage of the variation in holdings of "free" governments[5] are about what one would expect. In the definitional framework used by Bloch, however, one could interchange the accounts for "total bank loans" (an increase being a source of funds) and "free" governments (a decrease being a source of funds) and show that surpluses or deficits account for a similarly large percentage of variation in bank loans. This would follow, since Bloch shows the two accounts to serve as a source or use of funds to about the same extent, and since total sources are identically equal to total uses.

In symbolic terms, the essence of the above criticism may be restated. To do this, let us denote n separate sources of funds—$S_1, S_2, \ldots, S_n$—and m separate uses of funds—$U_1, U_2, \ldots, U_m$. Now, in an accounting framework, total sources always equal total uses.

(1) $S_1 + S_2 + \ldots + S_n = U_1 + U_2 + \ldots + U_m$

Next, let us denote S_n as so-called "free" governments; S_{n-1} as bank borrowing; and U_m as cash. Then

(2) $S_1 + S_2 + \ldots - U_1 - U_2 - \ldots - U_{m-1} = U_m - S_n - S_{n-1}$

Treating the left-hand member of equation (2) as constant—*const.* $= U_m - S_n - S_{n-1}$.

Now, an increase in U_m may be met from an increase in S_n and/or S_{n-1}. Bloch, in such a framework, finds that about 50 per cent of the change in U comes from a change in S_n. He concludes that government securities are

4. Early experience in such a framework illustrates a sources and uses statement for manufacturing corporations and shows the cash account to be relatively stable with other sources and uses evolving about it; see Frazer, "Suppliers of Funds," pp. 500-503.

5. Bloch, "Short Cycles," note 13.

the primary and predominating source of funds for adjusting the needs in cash for unknown future outlays. But, clearly, in this setting 50 per cent of the change in U_m is also accounted for by a change in S_{n-1}.

Government security holdings for "unknown" vs. planned future outlays.—Bloch's analysis indicates that short-run adjustments in the more stable cash account are affected primarily by changes in accounts pertaining to near money. These include the accounts for government securities and bank loans, to the extent that decreases in the indebtedness of firms at the bank are ready sources of cash for the firms in question. These latter accounts, however, have been shown to be major determinants of corporate liquidity broadly defined (Sec. 1.1), and corporate liquidity, in turn, has been shown elsewhere (Sec. 3.3) to be some increasing function of "planned capital outlays." These findings are in contrast to Bloch's statement (p. 1065) "that free governments serve as a financial reserve pool for *unknown* future investment outlays" (italics added).

Since results suggest that only some portion of government security holdings serve as a source of funds for planned expenditures on a specific backlog of projects, there is at times additional liquidity to be explained. As we show later (Chap. 7), the quarterly average for the ratio of government securities to bank loans for the entire corporate manufacturing sector declines by 23 per cent from 1958 to 1960, and a good bit of the decline can probably be explained by the greater certainty over future prospects in the postwar years as contrasted with earlier years. In other words, over the postwar years there was a decline in the need to hold money balances (and presumably near money), all relative to total assets and the flow of income, as a means of meeting "emergencies," "unforeseen opportunities," and in Bloch's words, for "unknown future investment outlays."

A summary of comments.—Professor Bloch has assumed two pools of government securities. One of these—"free" governments—served as a key variable in his discussion of the demand for government securities and money. He also attempts to give the variable "special" operational meaning by claiming that "free governments serve as a financial reserve pool for unknown future investment outlays." The data and statistical results in Tables 5-1 and 5-2, respectively, however, do not provide support for the strong Bloch assumption of two pools of governments. These findings, moreover, relate to other work, since others have used the notion of "free" governments. The comments also reveal that Bloch's emphasis in a "specific hypothesis" on free governments as a financial reserve pool could, in his own framework, have been placed upon bank loans (i.e., "immoneyness" or indebtedness at the bank). Finally, reviewing other findings, some government holdings were said to relate to *planned* investment outlays, and this relationship is partially in contrast to Professor Bloch's view whereby "free governments serve as a . . . pool for unknown future outlays."

5.2. THE "NEGLECTED" AND SOME OTHER FACTORS AFFECTING THE DEMAND FOR MONEY

In a January, 1964, article, Professor Richard H. Timberlake, Jr., concludes, "The role of financial non-money assets in monetary theory . . . would seem to be both quantitatively irrelevant and intellectually mischievous."[6] Earlier analysis (Sec. 1.1), on the other hand, suggests the prospect of a lack of support for Timberlake's conclusion, as it may apply to selected aspects of monetary analysis and the corporate manufacturing sector. Other findings (Sec. 3.1), moreover, deal with a factor that is reported by Timberlake as having been "neglected." This section, consequently, contains some of the previous findings pertaining to the "neglected" factor, tests of data concerning that factor, and specific instances of the inconsistency in Timberlake's conclusion and some empirical results. We do not, however, purport to deal with any of the questions about Timberlake's data, statistical tests, or criticisms of the Gurly-Shaw work. In fact, Professor Timberlake has published an admission of serious errors in his empirical work[7] subsequent to the publication of the article in question. This admission, nevertheless, has not altered his views about selected topics in monetary economics.

The "neglected" factor.—Timberlake cites "immoneyness" as the neglected factor concerning the demand for money. This factor, however, is dealt with in Sections 1.1, and 3.1 where bank loans, in particular, are viewed as a source of "illiquidity" or "immoneyness." It is also presently dealt with as a determinant of the income velocity of money. Namely,

$$\text{velocity (sales/cash)} = f\left(\frac{\substack{\text{government securities} \\ \text{(or non-cash liquid assets)}}}{\text{bank loans}}\right)$$

and given the omitted variables and parameters at a moment (or for a period) in time, $\dfrac{\partial \text{ velocity}}{\partial \text{ index of near moneyness}} > 0$. In this relationship, velocity is an increasing function of the index of near moneyness (Sec. 1.2), and bank loans enter as the denominator in the index. Increases in bank loans as they enter in the index comprise the "neglected" factor—Timberlake's "immoneyness."

6. "Stock of Money," p. 260.
7. See "The Stock of Money and Money Substitutes: Correction and Comment," *Southern Economic Journal*, Oct., 1964, pp. 149-52; David J. Ott, "The Stock of Money and Money Substitutes: Further Comment," *ibid.*, p. 153.

To deal with the relationship in question, data are tested and coefficients are reported concerning the following statement.

Velocity (sales/cash) is an increasing function of the ratio of government securities to bank loans for firms effecting a sizeable portion of cash adjustments through the money market.

The data analyzed include those for firms with asset in excess of 17.5 million dollars.[8] This lower bound was to exclude the smaller firms that were unlikely to effect frequent or no adjustments in their cash accounts through money market transactions (Sec. 7.2) as opposed to increments and decrements in indebtedness at the bank.

Some results of the linear approximations and the tests of data are summarized in Table 5-3, along with coefficients of determination. There we note that our special measure for velocity (sales/cash) is some increasing function of the ratio of government securities to bank loans. This is indicated by the presence of positive slope parameters for the linear approximation to the relationship in question for twenty quarters, following the first quarter of 1958. The slope parameters, moreover, become significantly different from zero, beginning in the third quarter of 1961. The slopes in the earlier years are less significant, in part, because of a sharp jump in the ratio of government security holdings of bank loans as one moves from firms between 250 to 1,000 million dollars in assets to those with assets over 1,000 million dollars.[9] A secular rise in velocity and a secular decline in the ratio combine,[10] however, to contribute to more significant slopes. The coefficients of determination, too, are shown to increase in response to this trend.

Additional aspects of monetary theory.—Timberlake outlines a fundamental aspect of monetary theory:

The liquidity preference demand for money that Keynes developed implies the existence of monetary assets that are not necessarily exchange media. Their hypothesized effect on the demand for money may be summarized as follows: Let the stock of relatively "safe" fixed claim debts increase [relative to the stock of money]. . . . The newly purchased assets do not effect any exchanges of goods and services

8. The classes considered were, in millions of dollars, 10 to 25, 25 to 50, 50 to 100, 100 to 250, 250 to 1,000, and over 1,000; thus, there were six "observations" and four degrees of freedom. Moreover, the slopes in Table 5-3 and in subsequent tables were tested for their significant difference from zero at the 10 per cent level of significance. This is because the tests were done as a part of a separate study and because I decided to take a greater chance on accepting an incorrect statement in view of the reduction in the number of degrees of freedom.

9. Tests of data show the slope parameters to be significantly different from zero for the earlier quarters when the largest class of firms is dropped.

10. From 1958 to 1960, both years of cyclical peaks, the quarterly average for velocity (sales/cash) increased approximately 54 per cent, for the entire corporate manufacturing sector, and the ratio of government securities to bank loans declined by 23 per cent.

but in satisfying the store-of-value function, they diminish the demand for money proper and increase the velocity of circulation. If this theory is relevant, the stock of marketable financial assets has significance in both monetary theory and monetary policy.[11]

He would apparently view the role of money substitutes in the latter theory as "quantitatively irrelevant and intellectually mischievous,"[12] as a result of his views and analysis. Apart from the detailed content and the particular emphasis on the store-of-value function, however, the above

TABLE 5-3

VELOCITY (SALES/CASH) WITH RESPECT TO THE RATIO OF
GOVERNMENT SECURITIES TO BANK BORROWING:
RESULTS FROM CROSS SECTION DATA FOR FIRMS
WITH OVER 10 MILLION DOLLARS IN ASSETS
(Seasonally adjusted)[1]

Year and Quarter[2]	COEFFICIENTS Regression (b)	Determination (r²)	Year and Quarter[2]	COEFFICIENTS Regression (b)	Determination (r²)
1958:			1961:		
			1 (trough)	0.16	0.13
2 (trough)	0.09	0.11			
3	0.12	0.20	3	0.30*	0.41
4	0.12	0.19	4	0.38*	0.49
1959:			1962:		
1	0.12	0.25	1	0.42*	0.48
2	0.09	0.19	2	0.33*	0.42
3	0.10	0.21	3	0.35*	0.47
4	0.13	0.27	4	0.39*	0.49
1960:			1963:		
1	0.17	0.28	1	0.44*	0.51
2 (peak)	0.16	0.30			
3	0.09	0.12			
4	0.12	0.11			

*Significantly different from zero at the 10 per cent level of significance.
1. The seasonal adjustment was effected by applying a four quarter moving average to the underlying data.
2. The terms "peak" or "trough" refer to turning points in the national business cycle as reported by the National Bureau of Economic Research.
Source: William J. Frazer, Jr., "Monetary Analysis and the Postwar Rise in the Velocity of Money in the United States," *Schweizerische Zeitschrift für Volkswirtschaft und Statistik*, December, 1964.

conclusion—the one whereby an increase in non-cash liquid assets increases the velocity of circulation—is supported by the prevalence of positive slopes for the linear approximations to the relationships for succeeding quarters between velocity (sales/cash) and the ratio of government securities to bank loans. Velocity and the latter ratio both increase as funds are released from cash to government securities. But this is via a relative weakening of the precautionary motive (Sec. 1.1), i.e., the release takes place as a result of a relative weakening of the demand for money "to

11. "Stock of Money," Jan., 1964, pp. 253-54.   12. *Ibid.*, p. 260.

hold as an asset . . . to meet subsequent liabilities fixed in terms of money," e.g., bank indebtedness. The theory in question is also consistent with the combination of statements 4 and 5 (Sec. 3.1) whereby government security holdings increase as cash decreases.

Elsewhere, Timberlake quotes Henry Thornton, an early British writer, as saying that bills of exchange (i.e., our non-cash liquid assets) are "at any time convertible into cash," and that "they render the supply of cash which is necessary to be kept in store much less considerable." Thornton's proposition is consistent with a combination of statements 4 and 5 and that concerning velocity (sales/cash). Apparently, from those statements, cash gets released to non-cash liquid assets and the process parallels a rise in the velocity of cash.

In conclusion, the findings pertaining to the slope parameters for linear approximations to the relationships for succeeding quarters do not provide a basis for rejecting the theoretical conclusion whereby an increase in non-cash liquid assets relative to the stock of money contributes to an increase in the velocity of circulation. Indeed, overall the statistical results outlined above provide some support for the monetary theory. These conclusions are contrary to some of Timberlake's.

The present comments in perspective.—In dealing with data concerning the velocity of money and moneyness in the form of non-cash liquid assets and a decrease in indebtedness at the bank, we are interested in (1) supporting or rejecting basic economic models (such as Keynes' version of the liquidity preference model), (2) determining the truth or untruth of statements about static and dynamic relationships implied by the models (such as "velocity . . . is an increasing function of the ratio of government securities to bank borrowing . . ."), and (3) using the latter results (a) to aid in the construction of simulation models of monetary phenomena occurring over time, and (b) to arrive at conclusions about the effectiveness of credit ease or tightness,[13] including the kind and extent of differential effects on different economic units.[14] Even so, at the present stage of monetary study there are problems. Where time is concerned, for example, we need quarterly data (of the type underlying the results in Table 5-3) that extend over a longer period of time in order to remove the secular variation. We also need to deal more competently with changes in different independent variables that are, in some instances, releasing balances to the transactions sphere and, in others, absorbing balances.

---

13. See, e.g., *ibid.*; Ritter, "Structure of Financial Markets," pp. 276-89; Friedman and Schwartz, *Monetary History,* Chap. 12; Ta-Chung Liu, "An Exploratory Quarterly Econometric Model of Effective Demand in the Postwar U.S. Economy," *Econometrica,* July, 1963, pp. 301-48; and references cited in the latter works.

14. See Frazer, "Financial Structure," p. 183.

Ideally, monetary economists would wish both macro and sectoral evidence from cross section data and the behavior of time series[15] over the short cycle, since the targets of the Federal Reserve's monetary operations and the explanations of monetary phenomena usually center about the short cycle. In actuality, on the other hand, the economists have: (1) used secular changes[16] to treat the implications of static models, (2) focused on changes over time in the absolute amount of government security holdings by the non-financial business sector with the view to generalizing about the economy as a whole,[17] and (3) and most of them have failed entirely to deal with the "neglected" factor.[18]

Further emphasis on the "neglected" factor and more evidence from time series data should contribute to greater success in the use of selected monetary models and in the testing of statements implied by them.

Summary of comments and some conclusions.—According to Keynes, as paraphrased by Timberlake, an increase in non-cash liquid assets diminishes "the demand for money proper and increases the velocity of circulation." According to Timberlake, on the other hand, the role of "non-money assets in monetary . . . theory would seem to be quantitatively irrelevant. . . ." My own studies, on the contrary, support the theoretical conclusions, although I reformulate the theory somewhat. In particular, cash is transferred to non-cash liquid assets and the velocity of circulation increases via a relative weakening of the precautionary motive.

Timberlake points out that "immoneyness" has been overlooked in studies concerning the demand for money. But my own analyses emphasize this factor in terms of the liquidity ratio and the ratio of government securities to bank loans. Viewing velocity (sales/cash) for those manufacturing firms most likely to deal in the money market, velocity appears to be an increasing function of the ratio of government securities to bank loans. An increase in bank loans, Timberlake's "immoneyness," therefore, reduces velocity, all in accordance with the results of tests of data.

Ideal support for statements implied by an aggregate model is not found in the present comments. The statistical results, nevertheless, emphasize the importance of a previously "neglected" factor, and contrary to a basic Timberlake conclusion, the results provide some support for a continuation of study and emphasis upon statements implied by Keynes' liquidity preference model, as outlined by Timberlake.

15. Stefan Valavanis, *Econometrics; An Introduction to Maximum Likelihood Methods* (New York: McGraw-Hill, 1959), pp. 192-95.
16. Timberlake does this; see "Stock of Money," pp. 255-60; and "Correction and Comment."
17. Ritter does this; see "Structure of Financial Markets," pp. 276-89.
18. Friedman and Schwartz fail in this respect (*Monetary History,* Chap. 12) as well as Ta-Chung Liu ("Econometric Model," p. 302, equation 1.1).

5.3. SUMMARY

Professor Ernest Bloch's analysis of the demand for money and government securities held by corporate manufacturing firms emphasizes a special category called "free" governments—i.e., government security holdings net of tax liabilities. He then proceeds to view the government security holdings in this category as the major means of effecting adjustments in the cash account. Among other things, he views this proof of liquid assets as being related to "unknown future investment outlays." Our statistical analyses, however, do not reveal support for the use of distinct pools of government securities such as "free" governments and "tax" governments. Also, in contrast to Bloch's view, firms' pools of liquidity have some relationship to planned capital outlays. Our review of his approach, further, indicates that he may just as well have emphasized the indebtedness of firms at the bank as a source of liquidity as "free" governments.

Bloch failed to deal explicitly with bank loans as an important means of effecting adjustments in the cash account and as a factor affecting the demand for cash. Indebtedness at the bank, in particular, has been referred to by Professor Timberlake as a "neglected" factor in analyses of the demand for money, but it has been emphasized in our overall approach to firms' demands for money. Timberlake, nevertheless, is critical of the role attributed to so-called money substitutes in monetary theory and policy. He has, in fact, cited some results from secular changes that lead him to view the role of so-called money substitutes in monetary theory as "quantitatively irrelevant and intellectually mischievous." Our own statistical findings, on the other hand, are consistent with that portion of Keynesian theory in which increasing near moneyness diminishes "the demand for money proper and increases the velocity of circulation." Indeed, there is some empirical support for the following statement:

Velocity (sales/cash) is an increasing function of the ratio of government securities to bank loans for firms effecting a sizeable portion of cash adjustments through the money market.

There is strong overall support for our general approach to firms' demand for money, government securities, and bank loans. This approach emphasizes the prevalence of a pool of liquidity that is affected by liquid asset holdings, bank loans, and the strength of the various motives for holding money. In particular, there is an apparent tendency for certain aspects of the precautionary demand for money balances to increase less than proportionally as asset size increases. This is apparently reflected in the additional tendency for the income velocity of money (i.e., the ratio of sales to cash in the present instance) to rise as firms begin to effect a sizeable portion of cash adjustments through the money market.

6. TRADE CREDIT AND MONETARY POLICY

The earlier analyses of data (Sec. 3.2) provided evidence of the likely independence of asset size and the ratio of accounts receivable to accounts payable for the corporate manufacturing sector. However, whenever one or more accounts are related in such a way as to be a net drain or a net source of cash (Sec. 2.1), they may have some effect on the velocity of money balances (i.e., the ratio of sales to the stock of cash in the present instance); and the accounts, furthermore, may be of interest to those who wish to deal with Federal Reserve credit policy in terms of the effects of changes in the money stock on expenditures and the turnover of money. In the case of trade credit, in particular, the earlier results (Sec. 3.2) appear to be somewhat in conflict with portions of Allan Meltzer's prominent work on trade credit and monetary policy, as we wish to show. Thus, in view of this prospect of some apparent conflict, as well as because of the similarities of our respective approaches and the common interest in the turnover of money balances, this chapter contains (1) a review of the findings about trade credit and the relevant aspects of the present approach, and (2) a review of some aspects of Meltzer's conclusions and approach.

Two Meltzer papers are involved—one appearing in 1960 and another in 1963.[1] They are referred to as his earlier (1960) and later (1963) work.

6.1. THE PRESENT APPROACH AND SOME STATISTICAL RESULTS

The present approach focuses upon the relationship between various sets of accounts as percentages of assets and/or income (i.e., sales). It does so (1) as a means of dealing with a common question in monetary economics as to whether some sets of accounts vary proportionally with total assets and/or income, and (2) as a means of utilizing certain analytical notions about changes in the scale of business operations. The present approach also involves sources and uses of funds (Sec. 2.1), and the statistical results shown throughout the essay rely upon data from the FTC-SEC's *Quarterly Financial Report*. All these latter features are present in varying degrees in the two Meltzer papers. The features in question are, consequently, briefly reviewed with emphasis on trade credit and the earlier Meltzer work.

The present approach.—In the present approach trade credit (Sec. 3.2) was related to asset size and sales. This relation was implied by the regression of the ratio of accounts receivable to accounts payable on asset size. The effects of size per se, such as a doubling of assets (Sec. 1.2), on

1. "Mercantile Credit," pp. 429-37; "Monetary Policy," pp. 471-97.

the changes in trade credit were avoided, and the analysis, instead, focused upon structural differences in firms by asset size. Now, in addition, one would expect manufacturing firms to add considerable value in the process of production to the goods and raw materials they receive. One would expect this to occur in such a way that the larger firms add more value per firm and accounts receivable exceed payables. All of this, moreover, would be consistent (1) with an expected increase in the absolute excess of accounts receivable over accounts payable as asset size and sales increase, and (2) with notions about a neutral credit or money policy. Such a policy would be one where the volume of bank credit, free reserves, and the stock of money vary in proportion with income (and assets) in such a way that money market rates of interest remain unchanged.[2] A tight money policy then becomes one where money and bank credit[3] rise less than in proportion to a rise in income, and interest rates rise; and an easy money policy becomes one where the money stock rises more than in proportion to income, and so on.

A review of statistical results.—Within the above framework the negative slope parameters (Sec. 3.2) suggest that the *larger* firms are inclined to extend *less* or use more trade credit than *smaller* firms, in relation to asset size, even though the slopes reveal only small differences from zero. It is these negative slopes and the apparent tendency for larger firms to extend smaller amounts of trade credit relative to their asset size that suggest some conflict between my results and some of Meltzer's conclusions. Namely, according to him, "(1) trade credit is a relatively important means of reallocating the existing money stock between large and small firms and (2) . . . the large (or liquid) firms lend to their smaller customers."[4] There is also another less directly involved point. Meltzer, on occasions, emphasizes bank credit as the origin of the funds to be redistributed, while I note that the larger firms are more independent of the need for bank credit and rely upon it to a smaller extent relative to their size (Sec. 3.1). On other occasions, nevertheless, he suggests the prospect of a redistribution of funds from non-bank sources.

Cross section data of the type analyzed earlier are shown in Table 6-1. There one may observe some properties of the data: (1) Accounts receivable exceed accounts payable as assumed above, as shown by the values (> 1) of the ratio for accounts receivable to accounts payable. (2) The two ratios (as percentages) reach a maximum for the 25 to 50 million

2. On the definitions, indicators, and concepts concerning monetary policy, see Frazer and Yohe, *Analytics and Institutions*, Secs. 2.3, 8.1, 20.2, 24.1, 24.2.

3. A rise in bank credit implies a rise in the stock of money but there are some intervening factors such as time-deposit drains that may cause some disparity in the bank-credit and money-supply changes; see Frazer and Yohe, Sec. 3.3.

4. "Monetary Policy," p. 473.

dollar asset size class, but the firms in this class fall within the lower 2.5 per cent of the domain over which the asset size variable may reasonably be defined (Sec. 1.2). (3) The two ratios for size class 1,000 million dollars and over are less than the corresponding ratios for the 1 to 5 million dollar size class and they are approximately equal to those for the smallest class of firms. Such facts as those under (2) and (3), and the fact that 1,000 million dollars is equal to or less than half of the domain for the firm size variable (Sec. 1.2), account for our negative slopes.

Changes in net receivables for selected years of cyclical expansion are shown in Table 6-2. One column of changes corresponds to the two-year

TABLE 6-1

RATIOS (AS PERCENTAGES) FOR ACCOUNTS RECEIVABLE TO
ACCOUNTS PAYABLE AND FOR NET RECEIVABLES[1] TO
SALES FOR FIRMS BY ASSET SIZE
END-OF-YEAR 1963

Size Class of Firms (in millions of dollars)	The Ratio (as a percentage) of Accounts Receivable to Accounts Payable	The Ratio (as a percentage) of Net Receivables to Sales
Under 1	1.45	.14
1 to 5	1.81	.21
5 to 10	2.32	.28
10 to 25	2.53	.33
25 to 50	(max.) 2.71	(max.) .36
50 to 100	2.63	.31
100 to 250	2.15	.30
250 to 1,000	1.89	.27
Over 1,000	1.52	.17

1. Net receivables refer to outstanding accounts and notes receivable less outstanding accounts and notes payable. The corresponding accounts in the FTC-SEC *Quarterly Financial Report* for the more recent years are, respectively, "other notes and accounts receivable (net)" and "trade accounts and notes payable."
Sources of data: U. S. Federal Trade Commission and Securities and Exchange Commission.

period 1954-56, and the second column of changes corresponds to the two-years period 1961-63. Data for the earlier years are shown because the period was covered by the Meltzer studies, and data for the latter years are shown because the data sources report a larger number of asset size classes. The data sources report nine classes by asset size for the more recent years and only seven for the earlier years as shown on the right and left hand sides of the table, respectively. With respect to these classes, the changes in net receivables over the years in question reveal that most classes of manufacturing corporations were, on balance, net sources of funds in the form of trade credit to other sectors, most likely including wholesale and retail businesses. Even the smallest classes of firms are shown to be net suppliers of retail credit.

It might be re-emphasized that we are dealing with the trade credit of manufacturing corporations independent of the practices of the sales finance subsidiaries of the very large firms (Sec. 3.2). The inclusion of such subsidiaries in the analyses of the data would not, however, affect major bases for our conclusions, since the firms in the asset size classes for the smaller firms do not reflect any special reliance upon trade credit, as a net source of funds, and since the role of the larger firms as suppliers of trade credit begins to diminish in relation to asset size with the size class 50 to 100 million dollars.

6.2. The Meltzer Process: Conflict and Resolution

Professor Meltzer is primarily concerned with structural changes over

TABLE 6-2

CHANGES IN THE RATIO OF RECEIVABLES TO SALES FOR FIRMS BY
ASSET SIZE DURING SELECTED YEARS OF CYCLICAL EXPANSION

Size Class of Firms (in millions of dollars)	Percentage Change— 4th Quarter 1954 to 4th Quarter 1956	Size Class of Firms (in millions of dollars)	Percentage Change— 4th Quarter 1961 to 4th Quarter 1963
Under .25	1.46		
.25 to 1	.04	Under 1	.12
1 to 5	— .25	1 to 5	.08
5 to 10	.16	5 to 10	— .03
10 to 50	— .03	10 to 25	.12
		25 to 50	.15
50 to 100	.20	50 to 100	.16
100 and over	.35	100 to 250	.37
		250 to 1,000	.36
		1,000 and over	.24

Sources of data: U. S. Federal Trade Commission and Securities and Exchange Commission.

time and with the prospect of some sort of restitution effect for small firms whereby the stock of bank credit in effect gets reallocated to smaller firms via the extension of trade credit to the small firms during periods of cyclical expansion. His studies deal mostly with the periods 1955-57 and 1954-58, respectively. He is writing, in part, in response to arguments that the rationing of credit by banks during periods of tight money favors large firms.[5] He has argued, "First, changes in velocity reallocate the existing and newly-created money stock among business firms. Second, the impact of tight money on small and large firms can be assessed only after the redistribution of asset holdings has taken place within the business sector."[6]

5. "Mercantile Credit," p. 429; "Monetary Policy," pp. 471-72, 477-78.
6. "Monetary Policy," p. 472.

The Meltzer Process.—The process set forth by Meltzer apparently works this way: "firms which accumulate liquid balances in periods of easy money use these balances to provide trade credit during periods of tight money."[7] To emphasize that firms' trade accounts make up a net source or use of funds during periods of tight money, and to call attention to the fact that such changes in trade credit are separate from those resulting from larger sales (or volume of business operations), Meltzer uses the ratio of net receivables (i.e., accounts receivable less accounts payable) to sales. He views liquid balances of large firms as a source of funds for the extension of trade credit to smaller firms, but continuing, he notes that "reductions in the cash balances of the largest firms during tight money contribute to a rise in velocity."[8] It is then in his later work that he says, "changes in velocity reallocate the existing and newly-created money stock among business firms" via changes in net receivables. He notes, among other things, that large (apparently 50 million dollars or more in assets) firms must "increase their outstanding net receivables proportionally more than their sales increase."[9]

Finally, with respect to the process, a crucial element is the length of the average collection period for trade credit. One expects trade credit to vary directly with sales (asset size, purchases, or scale of business operations), but if the use of trade credit by buyers is to increase more than in proportion to the rise in the volume of operations, then there must be an extension of the average collection period. Consequently, Meltzer sets forth factors influencing the allocation of trade credit,[10] cites a survey by Dun and Bradstreet on trade credit practices, indicates the likely existence of some "trade lenders," and presents a discriminant to aid in "identifying firms which lend to their customers by increasing their average collection period."[11]

Means of resolving the possible conflict.—Selected aspects of Meltzer's earlier work seem to conflict with some of my results, as indicated in the above review of statistical results (Sec. 6.1). Namely, linear approximations to cross section data reveal a decline in the ratio of accounts receivable to accounts payable as manufacturing corporations increase in size, and percentage changes over selected periods of cyclical expansion do not indicate that the smaller manufacturing corporations are net users of trade credit. In contrast, some of Meltzer's conclusions suggest that bank credit is being redistributed to the smaller manufacturing corporations via the net use of trade credit during periods of cyclical expansion.

---

7. "Mercantile Credit," p. 436.
8. *Ibid.*   9. "Monetary Policy," p. 472.
10. "Mercantile Credit," p. 431; see also Heston, "Empirical Study," pp. 124-25.
11. "Monetary Policy," pp. 486-93.

The reasons for the apparent conflict are these: (1) In the period covered by Meltzer's studies, only one asset size class was reported for firms with assets over 100 million dollars, as shown in Table 6-2. (2) Professor Meltzer has no special basis for distinguishing small firms as those with less than 50 million dollars in assets, and the majority of the asset size groups comprising firms under 50 million dollars reflect increases in their position as trade-lenders (Table 6-2).

In reference to the first reason, Meltzer could not observe the behavior of firms with assets over 100 million as separate groups. Now, in view of the increase in the number of classes, however, one may note (Table 6-1) that the ratio of net receivables to sales declines monotonically beginning with the asset class 50 to 100 million. In fact, for the asset class of 1,000 million and over, the ratio is below that for the asset class 1 to 5 million dollars. The ratios in Table 6-1 reflect stocks of trade credit, but these are the result of the accumulation of previous changes. Further, this explanation of the first reason for conflict, whereby Meltzer lacked access to the more recent data, would appear to be consistent with results from Meltzer's later work. Those results were based on a sample of 86 manufacturing corporations, and in the later work he rejects "high average liquidity position as a 'predictor' of trade lending."[12] On the other hand, I have noted that the largest firms in the nine-class breakdown for firms by asset size (Sec. 3.1) have the highest liquidity ratios.

In reference to the second reason for possible conflict between my results and Meltzer's, it should be pointed out that 50 million dollars covers only 2.5 per cent or less of the domain over which asset size may reasonably be defined for manufacturing corporations. Moreover, changes in the net payables position of the smallest firms by asset size reflect an enlargement of their position as trade lenders during periods of cyclical expansion—as shown in Table 6-2, and in Meltzer's own results.[13] In the light of the overall view of my results and Meltzer's work on trade credit, Meltzer is apparently focusing upon a process that is more prevalent in dealings between manufacturing corporations and other firms than between firms within the corporate manufacturing sector. In fact, in his later work on

12. "Monetary Policy," p. 479.

13. Where R is the ratio of net receivables to sales and S is an index of seasonally adjusted sales, Meltzer's results for the period covering the first quarter 1954 to the fourth quarter 1957 contain the following.

Size Class (in millions of dollars)	$\partial R/\partial S$
Under .25	.09
.25 to 1	.19
1 to 5	−.01
5 to 10	−.19
10 to 50	−.28

The positive coefficients $\partial R/\partial S$ are biased downward according to "Mercantile Credit," pp. 432-33.

trade credit, he emphasizes "that a principal direction of change was from corporate to non-corporate firms."[14] The tendency for net receivables as proportions of sales to rise in years of cyclical expansion, as in Table 6-2, clearly reflects a net extension of trade credit, quite likely to wholesale and retail firms, but the tendency for the mass of the latter firms to be relatively small, as well as different in other respects, should not be interpreted as being inconsistent with my statistical results.

Meltzer's two points, stated earlier, that changes in velocity reallocate the money stock and that "the impact of tight money on small and large firms can be assessed only after the redistribution of asset holdings has taken place" can also be stated in other words. Namely, in order to assess more fully the impact of tight money on the various sectors, we must examine changes in the financial structure of the units comprising various sectors and their responses to conditions in the financial markets. This is the way we have been proceeding.

In this chapter, I have, in part, sought (1) to put forth some bases for a possible conflict between Meltzer's conclusions about trade credit and my statistical results from cross section data and (2) to indicate bases for resolving the possible conflict.

6.3. SUMMARY

The present emphasis is upon certain aspects of firms' demands for money, bank loans, and government securities. This is, in part, because of the role of liquidity in monetary economics; and it is, in part, because the analyses of data showed these accounts to vary more significantly in relation to changes in asset size than other accounts. Nevertheless, other accounts may serve as a source or use of money balances and exercise some effect on the turnover of such balances, and, as a consequence, they may be of interest to those who wish to deal with the effectiveness of changes in the stock of money on expenditures. In particular, some research by Allan Meltzer has focused upon such changes, and portions of Meltzer's reports on the research appear on the surface to conflict, primarily, with the results from linear approximations to cross section data for the ratio of accounts receivable to accounts payable and firms by asset size. They also appear to conflict, to a lesser extent, with present notions about the relative independence of large firms from banks.

Meltzer's work on trade credit focuses upon changes in the ratio of net receivables (i.e., receivables less payables) to sales for the manufacturing sector as a means of dealing with a number of questions—some about the possible discriminatory effect of general credit controls on small firms, and some about the allocation and redistribution of bank credit via changes

14. "Monetary Policy," pp. 473,493.

in the ratio of net receivables to sales. Meltzer arrives at a number of conclusions: Small firms are net receivers of trade credit from large firms during periods of tight money; the drain on cash by the increase in net receivables for large firms contributes to a rise in the turnover of their money balances; changes in the velocity of money balances serve to redistribute new and existing money balances in favor of the smaller firms; and the redistribution effect of changes in velocity or, more directly, changes in net receivables must be allowed for in assessing the impact of a tight money policy.

The conflict between the Meltzer conclusions and the present findings, however, are more apparent than real. Taking an overall view—making allowances for both the data originally at Meltzer's disposal and later results from cross section data—the redistribution effects via net receivables appear to work mainly through the relationships between manufacturing firms and wholesale and retail firms rather than within the corporate manufacturing sector. The tendency for the mass of wholesale and retail firms to be small relative to manufacturing firms should not obscure the fact that the Meltzer process applies mainly to relationships between the corporate manufacturing sector and the sectors receiving its products rather than between firms in the corporate manufacturing sector itself. In order to assess more fully the impact of tight money on the various sectors and, thus, ultimately the impact (Sec. 8.2) upon national income, the level of employment, and the average of prices, we must examine, among other things, changes in the financial structure of the units comprising the various sectors and their responses to changes in the stock of money.

7. MONEY! A "LUXURY" GOOD?

In their monumental work, Milton Friedman and Anna Jacobson Schwartz view money as a "luxury" good. According to their view,[1] "the services rendered by money balances" are "a 'luxury' of which the amount demanded rises more than in proportion to the rise in income" and presumably assets. Thus, they use the term "luxury" to connote the velocity of money as a decreasing function of income (and presumably total assets) for the economy as a whole, as well as for the non-financial business sector,[2] although they would recognize a rise in the velocity of

1. *Monetary History of the United States*, p. 639.
2. *Ibid.*, p. 643. Friedman and Schwartz affirm their feeling about the applicability of the "luxury goods" hypothesis to the business sector in the following note (note 12, p. 654): "Selden suggests in his article on velocity by sectors that the

money, as well as income, during the postwar years, and attribute the rise in velocity to a weakening of a certain form of the precautionary motive (Sec. 1.1) for holding money.[3] In contrast, statistical tests of cross section data and conclusions presented above (e.g., Sec. 5.2) and in a previous article by me[4] suggest that the turnover of money by the corporate manufacturing sector is an increasing function of asset size. For example, one conclusion was that "an effect of increasing firm size is to pull the less active precautionary balances into the more active transactions sphere, at least with respect to capital expenditures."

In this earlier conclusion, there is the suggestion that money balances are used more economically as firms increase in size. Proceeding with this suggestion, then, the proposition is submitted that the velocity of money is an increasing function of asset size, at least over the major portion of the domain for the asset size variable for manufacturing corporations, and under the conditions characterized by institutions of the later post-World-War-II years.

Friedman and Schwartz review secular trends. Even so, I wish to show that our conflicting hypotheses, as applied to current times and the business sector, may be accounted for on other grounds.[5] In particular, given the wide range of factors Friedman and Schwartz deal with, especially in explaining the post-World-War-II rise in the velocity of money,[6] they fail to deal with a significant aspect of the precautionary motive for holding money as set forth by Keynes. A practical result of this failure is to leave unexplained some of the postwar rise in the velocity of money, as I wish to illustrate.

In proceeding, I review the following: Keynes on the precautionary motive, an overlooked part of the definition of the precautionary motive,

---

operation of the income effect is limited to households only. This may be so. However, it is not at all clear that it is. Money balances may be a factor of production, the marginal productivity of which rises relative to other factors with an expansion of scale of both the individual enterprise and the economy. Seldon's own cross-section data on firms of different sizes suggest that money balances have this property (see Selden, *Postwar Rise in the Velocity*, pp. 500-502, and 524, footnote 24."

3. This weakening of the precautionary motive could be interpreted as an upward shift in the function relating the income velocity of money to income.

4. "Financial Structure," pp. 176-83.

5. For a brief discussion of cross section versus time series estimates see Valavanis, *Econometrics*, pp. 192-95; he makes the point that discrepancies in estimates of behavioral functions—the consumption function in his case and the money-demand function in the present case—from cross section as opposed to time series data are not due to attempts to measure different kinds of behavior. For another note on the relationship between time series and cross section estimates, see Meltzer, "Reply," *Quarterly Journal of Economics*, Feb., 1965, p. 164.

6. *Monetary History*, pp. 639-75.

the demand for money by manufacturing corporations and tests of cross section data, and factors contributing to the post-World-War-II rise in velocity according to Friedman and Schwartz.

7.1. THE PRECAUTIONARY MOTIVE ONCE AGAIN

The precautionary motive as stated by Keynes (Sec. 1.1) concerned the holding of cash "to provide for [1] contingencies requiring sudden expenditures and for unforeseen opportunities of advantageous purchases, and also [2] to hold an asset of which the value is fixed in terms of money to meet a subsequent liability [e.g., bank loans] fixed in terms of money." Friedman and Schwartz appear to deal exclusively with the first of these concerns, in discussing the precautionary motive for holding money and its effects on the velocity of money. They say,

> After all, the major virtue of cash as an asset is its versatility. It involves a minimum of commitment and provides a maximum of flexibility to meet emergencies and to take advantage of opportunities. The more uncertain the future, the greater the value of such flexibility and hence the greater the demand for money is likely to be.[7]

Apparently they are elaborating on the precautionary motive as it concerns "contingencies" and "unforeseen opportunities." I, on the other hand, have attributed some importance to the second of the above concerns. More specifically,[8] I have advanced a notion that "the precautionary demand does not increase proportionally with wealth . . . as wealth rises." This led to the conjecture that an "effect of increasing firm size . . . was to pull the less active precautionary balances into the more active transactions sphere." I viewed this in terms of the tendency for both cash as a percentage of assets and bank loans as a percentage of assets (or liabilities) to decline as asset size increases. This tendency is consistent, too, with the banking practice of requiring the maintenance of compensating money balances on deposit as some percentage of the amount of borrowed funds,[9] although the latter practice is not really an issue in the present context.

7. *Ibid.*, pp. 673-75. Their statistical definition of money is slightly different from the present one. Money is presently viewed as the sum of "currency held by the public and demand deposits adjusted," whereas they (p. 630) view money as the "total of currency held by the public plus demand and time deposits adjusted in commercial banks." This difference should cause no great problem, however, especially since (1) the present data for the money stocks held by corporations are from balance sheets, and likely include any time deposits held by corporations, and (2) Friedman and Schwartz show the respective series to vary in the same direction anyway (p. 631).

8. "Financial Structure," p. 177.

9. On compensating balances, see Frazer and Yohe, *Analytics and Institutions,* Sec. 14.2.

7.2. THE DEMAND FOR MONEY AND SOME STATISTICAL FINDINGS

In recent years a good bit has been written about the demand for money, including the demand by the non-financial business sector.[10] Most of this work, however, has neglected to deal with the second part of the definition of the precautionary motive, as stated above, and, at the same time, it has failed to treat decreases in bank loans as a source of near money. Thus, to deal with the Friedman-Schwartz view of money as a "luxury good," as well as to deal with the question of the importance of the "neglected factors," the results from tests of data concerning the "luxury goods" hypothesis and the presumed relation between income and total assets are summarized, a proposition is then advanced, and additional results from tests of data concerning the proposition are summarized. Before getting to these matters, however, some questions are dealt with concerning the distinction between so-called large (or money market) firms, and the presence of economies in the management of cash.

Following the Friedman-Schwartz usage, "luxury good" in the present context may simply refer to the velocity of money as a decreasing function of income (asset size or wealth). Some may "regard the holding of larger-than-necessary cash balances as a luxury" with the view that "perhaps an increase in real income would produce a larger-than-proportional increase in the demand for money."[11] The net result of this use of the terms "larger-than-necessary" and "luxury," nevertheless, is a decline in the velocity of money in relation to a rise in real income, and we may in the present instance accept this latter result as evidence of money's being a luxury good without attaching any special sensuous meaning to the terms "larger-than-necessary" and "luxury."

Money market firms and the turnover of money balances.—Firms are small or large in relation to one another. In this sense, an objective stand-

10. See the references in the works presently cited, and in Bloch, "Short Cycles," pp. 1058-77; the latter work, especially, emphasizes the role of government security holdings by the corporate manufacturing sector, and the importance of the sector in determining the demand for government securities and money for the economy as a whole.

11. William S. Vickrey, *Metastatics and Macroeconomics* (New York: Harcourt, Brace, 1964), p. 84; on the demand for money, the volume of transactions, and business firms, we may quote Professor Vickrey: "Doubling the volume of transactions will double the minimum amount of money needed to perform them without running into an absolute shortage of cash and an increase in income will be likely to produce a roughly corresponding increase in the amount of money held to meet contingencies. To some extent, if we regard the holding of larger-than-necessary cash balances as a luxury, perhaps an increase in real income would produce a larger-than-proportional increase in the demand for money; however, since a large proportion of cash balances is held by firms where this luxury aspect of the matter would be of less importance, the proportionality assumption still seems warranted, at least as a rough first approximation."

ard for distinguishing small from large firms would doubtlessly involve the domain over which asset size may reasonably be defined. Earlier (Sec. 1.2) this domain for regression purposes was viewed as being roughly between zero and 2,000 million dollars for the late post-World-War-II years.[12] By such a standard, however, firms of even 75 to 100 million dollars in assets would be small, since they would fall within the lower 5 per cent of the domain of definition. Thus, I propose to distinguish by asset size a group of firms to be referred to as money market firms. These I view as those firms that appear to begin to effect some economy in the use of cash by availing themselves of sources of near cash such as government security holding and relatively small amounts of indebtedness at the bank in relation to their size, although such firms may have only very indirect contact with dealers in the New York government securities and money market.[13] Earlier analyses (Sec. 3.1) lead to the emphasis on government securities and bank loans for two reasons: (1) apart from cash, government securities and bank loans were the accounts that were most affected by changes in size, and (2) findings indicate that firms as they increase in size effect a greater use of government security holdings as a source of cash and a relatively smaller use of bank loans in relation to their size.

In focusing on the ratio of government securities to bank loans and the notion that the added liquidity from government securities permits a more economical use of money balances (i.e., a faster turnover), I arrive at the point 17.5 million dollars (i.e., the mid-point of the asset size class 10 to 25 million) or 15.4 (i.e., the mean size for the size class 10 to 25 million) as the point for distinguishing between money market and other firms. I do this because the turnover of cash begins to increase for firms in this class on the average (see Table A-1 in the Appendix to this chapter). One might note, too (Table A-2), that the ratio of government securities to bank loans (as a percentage) increases fairly consistently, beginning with the smallest class of firms.

Apparently the relatively small firms operate under rather stringent conditions concerning the availability of cash, and thus exercise some "luxury" in its use up to approximately 17.5 million dollars, using the mid-point of a size class, or up to 15.4, using the mean size. Beyond this, economies in the management of cash set in, and a more expert management becomes possible with cash adjustments being effected in the money market and through increases and decreases in bank loans.

---

12. The domain would vary over time with the growth of firms. The one we have selected (notes 19, 20, Sec. 1.2) by rather crude means may be considered satisfactory for the median years for which data are analyzed.

13. On these markets see Frazer and Yohe, Chap. 13, 14.

The economies in question, however, are those relating to the effective use of cash rather than to dollar and cents savings. This may be shown from an assessment of the major costs involved in effecting a financial structure resulting in increases in the turnover of money balances for an average firm in the 10 to 25 million size class. Using 4th-quarter 1963 data, for example, the turnover of money balances would increase by about 50 per cent as the average size firm in question took on the financial structure of the average size firm in the 1,000 million dollar and over size class. Or, looking at the matter another way, the latter rise in velocity is equivalent to a one-third reduction in the size of the cash account for the average size firm in the 10 to 25 asset size class. Thus, using earlier analysis and 1963 data (Secs. 3.1, 3.2), the structural change would call for a transfer of 3.7 per cent of assets from cash to government securities and possibly a small additional increase in government securities. The decrease in cash would, of course, parallel a reduction in bank loans as a percentage of assets and the need for cash, part of which would now be met from the rise in government security holdings. The decrease in bank loans for this purpose would be in the magnitude of 6.7 per cent of total assets or about 5.7 per cent after the allowance for a small additional increase in governments. The funds for the latter decrease in bank loans would come largely from an increase in owners' equity of 5.6 per cent of total assets.

Thus, with these structural changes in mind, the net cost of effecting a 50 per cent increase in velocity may be estimated for an average firm with 15.4 million dollars in assets. In such a case, the gross cost would be mainly, let us say, a 12 per cent return (after corporate taxes) on the extra equity or about .1 million dollars per annum. The savings per annum would be about .04 million on bank loans at 4 per cent, and there would be an income on the extra governments of about .02 million at a 3 per cent return per annum. Therefore, there is a net cost for realizing a 50 per cent increase in the velocity of cash of about .08 million dollars for the average firm in the 10 to 25 asset size class. As a firm actually increased in size there would be economies in unit costs resulting from the specialization in financial management, transactions costs,[14] and so on, but these savings would be nominal relative to the costs mentioned; and the latter, moreover, would be a sort of minimum cost since the absolute cost of achieving the more liquid structure would increase with actual size. Apparently, there are no net dollar and cents economies in taking on a

14. For a discussion of economies in transactions costs on government securities see Heston, "Empirical Study," p. 212. On transactions costs in short-term government securities, see also James S. Duesenberry, "The Portfolio Approach to the Demand for Money and Other Assets," *Review of Economics and Statistics*, Supplement: "The State of Monetary Economics," 1963, pp. 12-13.

financial structure typical of the largest firms. The structure of the larger firms is a more liquid one, nevertheless, and apparently managers of these firms attach a considerable value—even though a subjective one—to the extra liquidity. There is a convenience and security for which they are willing to pay something.

Clearly, the "wealth effect" holds for the overall liquidity structure— i.e., corporate liquidity (Sec. 3.1) is an increasing function for firms by asset size. And, in this case, the view is more in accord with that of Friedman and Schwartz. However, as asset size and liquidity increase, the precautionary motive of type 2 comes into play. As bank loans in relation to assets decline, cash in relation to assets declines. The luxury goods hypothesis simply does not hold for money, although the hypothesis (or equivalently, the "asset size effect" in this case) applies to the overall liquidity structure.

Velocity: An increasing function of asset size.—The above evidence— that the least efficient use of cash occurs at a relatively small asset size— suggests the following statement:

1. Velocity (the dollar volume of sales to cash)[14a] increases as firms increase in size, at least beyond some minimum. This minimum might be thought of as occurring when financial managers begin to become specialists or, at least, at a sufficiently early stage to allow the statement to be true over the predominant portion of the scale for asset size.

Some results of a linear approximation to data concerning this relationship and coefficients of determination are summarized in Table 7-1. There one may note that the slope parameters are all positive and significantly different from zero. One may also note that a good portion of the variation in velocity is explained by increases in asset size and presumably sales or income. The tests and coefficients of regression and determination, as summarized in Table 7-1, are strong evidence in support of statement 1. Statement 1, moreover, is in contrast to the Friedman-Schwartz hypothesis about money's being a "luxury" good.

Income (or sales): A function of asset size.—An increase in income (or sales), in lieu of an increase in asset size in statement 1, would also give rise to an increase in velocity. At least, earlier findings indicate that assets and income vary directly (Sec. 3.1), and Friedman and Schwartz state the "luxury good" hypothesis with income as the independent variable.

14a. Changes in the ratio of sales to cash are used as a substitute measure for changes in the corporate manufacturing sector's component for income velocity (Sec. 8.2). Admittedly some double counting is involved in equating sales to the contribution of manufacturing corporations to GNP. Changes in income velocity are usually of greater interest to economists, however, than changes in other measures of velocity.

Velocity and the definition of the precautionary motive: A proposition.—The proposition, with which I wish to deal is as follows: *An effect of increasing firm size over the predominant portion of the domain for firms by asset size is to pull the less active precautionary balances into the more active transactions sphere and thus to give rise to an increase in the velocity of money.*

This follows from a previously presented statement (Sec. 3.1), a previously stated assumption (Sec. 1.1), and that part of the definition of the

TABLE 7-1

VELOCITY (SALES/CASH) WITH RESPECT TO ASSET SIZE:
RESULTS FROM CROSS SECTION DATA FOR FIRMS
WITH OVER $10 MILLION IN ASSETS

(Seasonally adjusted)[1]

Year and Quarter[2]	COEFFICIENTS Regression (b)	COEFFICIENTS Determination (r^2)	Year and Quarter[2]	COEFFICIENTS Regression (b)	COEFFICIENTS Determination (r^2)
1958:			1961:		
2 (trough)	0.0006*	0.51	1 (trough)	0.0006*	0.44
3	0.0007*	0.61	2	0.0008*	0.63
4	0.0010*	0.61	3	0.0010*	0.75
1959:			4	0.0011*	0.83
1	0.0010*	0.58	1962:		
2	0.0008*	0.51	1	0.0013*	0.81
3	0.0008*	0.54	2	0.0015*	0.79
4	0.0009*	0.60	3	0.0013*	0.83
1960:			4	0.0014*	0.84
1	0.0009*	0.61	1963:		
2 (peak)	0.0009*	0.65	1	0.0016*	0.84
3	0.0008*	0.39			
4	0.0005*	0.41			

*Significantly different from zero at the 10 per cent level of significance (see note 14, Sec. 5.2).
1. The seasonal adjustment was effected by applying a four-quarter moving average to the underlying data.
2. The terms "peak" and "trough" refer to turning points in the national business cycle as reported by the National Bureau of Economic Research.
Source: Frazer, "Monetary Analysis and the Postwar Rise in the Velocity of Money in the United States," *Schweizerische Zeitschrift für Volkswirtschaft und Statistik*, Dec., 1964.

precautionary motive concerning an asset "to meet a subsequent liability." The previously presented statement is that the proportion of assets in the form of government securities varies directly with asset sizes[15] and, presumably, income, in view of earlier findings (Sec. 3.1). Next, the previous assumption being relied upon is that non-cash liquid assets have provided a partial substitute for the increases in and repayment of bank debt

15. The statement, too, would apparently be in accord with the Friedman-Schwartz hypothesis (p. 660) where "wealth holders" have come to hold more money substitutes relative to other assets.

as a means of effecting adjustments in the cash account. Thus, as assets (and income) increase, the proportion of assets held in non-cash liquid assets increases, bank loans relative to total assets decline, and by the second part of the definition of the precautionary motive the above proposition becomes plausible.

Empirical support for the proposition.—To provide empirical support

TABLE 7-2

THE RATIO OF GOVERNMENT SECURITIES TO BANK BORROWING
WITH RESPECT TO ASSET SIZE: RESULTS FROM CROSS SECTION
DATA FOR FIRMS WITH OVER $10 MILLION IN ASSETS
(Seasonally adjusted)[1]

Year and Quarter[2]	COEFFICIENTS Regression (*b*)	COEFFICIENTS Determination (*r²*)	Year and Quarter[2]	COEFFICIENTS Regression (*b*)	COEFFICIENTS Determination (*r²*)
1958:			1961:		
			1 (trough)	0.0026*	0.88
2 (trough)	0.0025*	0.77	2	0.0025*	0.88
3	0.0033*	0.79	3	0.0025*	0.87
4	0.0041*	0.81	4	0.0026*	0.87
1959:			1963:		
1	0.0050*	0.87	1	0.0026*	0.86
2	0.0053*	0.87	2	0.0027*	0.85
3	0.0048*	0.87	3	0.0027*	0.85
4	0.0042*	0.87	4	0.0026*	0.86
1960:			1963:		
1	0.0037*	0.87	1	0.0026*	0.86
2 (peak)	0.0032*	0.87			
3	0.0030*	0.87			
4	0.0027*	0.87			

*Significantly different from zero at the 10 per cent level of significance.
1. The seasonal adjustment was effected by applying a four-quarter moving average to the underlying data.
2. The terms "peak" and "trough" refer to turning points in the national business cycle as reported by the National Bureau of Economic Research.
Source: Frazer, "Monetary Analysis and the Postwar Rise in the Velocity of Money in the United States," *Schweizerische Zeitschrift für Volkswirtschaft und Statistik*, Dec., 1964.

for the proposition, data for manufacturing corporations are tested concerning one additional statement:

2. The ratio of government securities and similar non-cash liquid assets to bank loans increases as firms increase in asset size. This statement, as one may note, combines the government securities variable in an earlier statement with the bank loans variable of an earlier notion, as reviewed above.

The data pertaining to statement 2 are presented in Table A-2, and the tests of data concerning relationship 2, and the coefficients for the linear approximation to data concerning that relationship are summarized in Table 7-2. These results of the tests provide strong evidence that statement 2 is true, and the coefficients of determination indicate that a major portion of the ratio of government securities to bank loans is explained in terms of firms by asset size.

Statements 1 and 2 suggest that velocity is an increasing function of the ratio of government securities to bank loans, at least for firms with assets over 17.5 million dollars. Thus, as a logical result of the statements 1 and 2, a third statement follows:

3. Velocity increases as the ratio cited in statement 2 increases, at least over the predominant portion of the domain of firms by asset size. This is the statement that the proposition itself leads us to make.

Tests and coefficients supporting such a statement, moreover, were outlined earlier in Table 5-3.[15a] From Table 5-3 one notes that the regression coefficients for the linear approximations are all positive, and that some of the rise in velocity is explained by the ratio of government security holdings to bank loans. Beginning in the 3rd-quarter 1961, in fact, the slope parameters become significantly different from zero.[16] The lack of significantly high slopes before 1961 is, in part, due to the large jump in the ratio as firms increase from between 250 to 1,000 million dollars in asset size to over 1,000 million. This factor is overcome, however, as the ratio tends to decline and velocity to rise, over the years 1958-63.

The tests of data corresponding to the variables mentioned in statements 2 and 3, and statement 1 as well, and the slopes of the linear approximations to the relationships between variables, all combine to give empirical support to the proposition in question. Apparently, an effect of increasing firm size beyond some minimum (of approximately 17.5 million dollars) is to pull balances into the transactions sphere, via the second part of the definition of the precautionary motive as restated at the outset.

7.3. THE POSTWAR RISE IN VELOCITY

Over the postwar years some circumstances have given rise to an increase in income velocity of money. One set of these is supported by the Friedman-Schwartz study,[17] and two others are mentioned as being cited by most students. As the analysis and empirical results have shown, however, there is more or less of a rise to be explained by the second part of

15a. Results from the analysis of cross section data for industry groups of firms by asset size provide some additional support for the behavior attributed to the ratio of sales to cash with respect to asset size. As reported elsewhere (Meltzer, "The Demand for Money: A Cross-Section Study of Business Firms," *Quarterly Journal of Economics*, Aug., 1963, p. 416), there is a tendency for cash to rise more than in proportion to sales for industries populated by small firms, and there is a tendency among a larger group of industries for cash to rise less than in proportion to sales.

16. Additional tests showed they were also significantly different from zero prior to the 3rd-quarter 1961, when the largest class size was dropped.

17. *Monetary History*, pp. 644-45.

the definition of the precautionary motive. Whether more or less depends, in the above context, on (1) whether the ratio of government security holdings to bank loans has declined or risen, and on (2) the extent to which this ratio, operating via the precautionary motive for holding money, is dealt with in other studies. If the ratio has declined, it has deactivated balances, and the other factors must be shown to have contributed to the actual rise in velocity as well as that portion absorbed by the decline in the ratio of government securities to bank loans. In this case, there is more to be accounted for. If the ratio has risen, on the other hand, then there is less to be explained by other factors since a rise in the ratio released balances to the more active transactions sphere for the corporations in question. To put these matters in perspective, we review briefly (1) the changes in key variables over the postwar years, (2) the Friedman-Schwartz review of the relevant circumstances as emphasized by their study and by others, and (3) an omission from the Friedman-Schwartz study.

Changes in key variables.—From 1948 to 1960, two postwar years in which cyclical peaks were reached, the following approximate changes occurred in key variables:

THE ECONOMY AS A WHOLE

Total gross national product (or income) *increased*	94 per cent
The money supply[18] *increased*	27 per cent
Income velocity, as indicated by the variables underlying the latter changes, *increased*	53 per cent

THE CORPORATE MANUFACTURING SECTOR

The quarterly average of sales *increased*	109 per cent
The average end-of-quarter cash holdings *increased*	29 per cent
The quarterly average for velocity (sales/cash) *increased*	54 per cent
The quarterly average for the ratio of government securities to bank loans *declined*	23 per cent

Note that the changes for the entire economy correspond roughly in magnitude to the changes for the corporate manufacturing sector. The additional change for the ratio of government securities to bank loans is used as an indicator of the extent of change in near moneyness (Sec. 1.1).

The Friedman-Schwartz review.—Friedman and Schwartz review two sets of circumstances by which most students attempt to explain the postwar rise in velocity. They also present a third set. It is, briefly stated:[19] "(1) A greater rise in the return on alternative assets than in the net direct return on money. . . . (2) A reduction in the value attached to monetary services because of institutional changes which have created closer substitutes for money than formerly existed. . . . (3) A decline in

18. The money supply change is estimated from averages of daily December figures. It is statistically defined as demand deposits plus currency.
19. *Monetary History*, pp. 644-45.

the value attached to monetary services because of changed expectations of holders of money about the likely degree of future economic stability."

The third of these sets of circumstances is supported by the Friedman-Schwartz study as an explanation of the postwar rise in velocity. Apparently, this set, along with the first, has some support. It is essentially circumstances operating via the first aspect of the precautionary motive as set forth above (Sec. 7.1).

A Friedman-Schwartz omission.—In their discussion concerning the possible relationships between so-called money substitutes and a rise in velocity,[20] Friedman and Schwartz do not deal with a decline in bank loans as a percentage of asset size as an important money substitute. In other words, the institutional practice of increasing the ratio of government securities to bank loans as firms increased in size is not mentioned as a factor affecting income velocity. The relevance of this omission, however, is indicated by the above analysis. Namely, the practice of adjusting cash needs through bank loans (i.e., the repayment and subsequent increase in bank debt) declines as the practice of effecting changes in cash needs through adjustments in non-cash liquid assets increases, as firms increase in size over the relevant domain. And in the present paper velocity is an increasing function of the ratio of government security holdings to bank loans, at least as the ratio relates directly to the precautionary motive of type 2 as set forth earlier (Sec. 1.1) and as restated above.

With reference to the changes in key variables over the postwar years as cited above, one notes that the ratio of government securities to bank loans declined. Thus, given the functional relationship established earlier, it apparently absorbed active balances. Consequently, there is more of the postwar rise in velocity to be explained than one finds explained by current studies. The secular changes in other key variables—namely, sales, cash holdings, and velocity—for the corporate manufacturing sector were apparently reflected in the secular changes for the economy as a whole; the corresponding variables for the entire economy show secular changes in the same direction and to about the same extent as those from the corporate sector.

7.4 SUMMARY

Milton Friedman and Anna Jacobson Schwartz view money as a "luxury" good. By this they mean that the velocity of money declines as wealth increases. They hold this view, both with respect to the entire economy and with respect to the nonfinancial business sector. My own findings, on the other hand, do not support this view as it applies to the corporate manufacturing sector. Instead, they support the proposition that the

20. *Monetary History*, pp. 659-60.

amount of money demanded rises less than in proportion to the rise in income (and assets) for the strategic sector of manufacturing corporations, at least as asset size (and sales) increase beyond some minimum size. This size is presumed to occur at some stage where financial management becomes a specialized function. At that stage, economies in the utilization of cash set in, apparently because of the practice of effecting adjustments in the cash account through the money market.

To deal empirically with the question of whether the turnover of cash balances decreases (or increases) as asset size increases for firms in the manufacturing sector a number of steps were taken: linear approximations were made to various relationships, and a proposition was presented. The proposition emphasized that money balances are drawn into the more active transactions sphere as firms increase in asset size. This phenomenon was related to the precautionary motive for holding money balances. The various linear approximations to cross section data, slope parameters, and coefficients of determination, all taken together, indicate the following, for asset sizes in excess of 17.5 million dollars: (1) velocity (sales/cash) varies directly with asset size (and presumably income); (2) asset size varies directly with sales (or income), and, for large firms in general, an increase in assets results in an equal increase in sales; (3) the ratio of government securities to bank loans, as a measure of near moneyness, varies directly with asset size; and (4) velocity varies directly with the latter measure for near moneyness. The first and second of the statements in the latter list and the tests of data pertaining to both statements support the view whereby the amount of money demanded rises less than in proportion to the rise in asset size. The entire list of statements supports the above proposition, including the claim about the relevance of the precautionary motive. Friedman and Schwartz, moreover, are said to overlook the relevance of the ratio of government securities to bank loans in explaining the postwar rise in velocity. This ratio is shown to have offset some of the rise in velocity that would have occurred had the ratio remained constant. Thus, in a sense, there is more than the apparent increase in velocity to be explained.

APPENDIX TO CHAPTER 7

DATA (SEASONALLY ADJUSTED) FOR THE TURNOVER OF CASH AND THE INDEX OF NEAR MONEYNESS

The seasonally adjusted data that were analyzed in the text are contained in the two tables comprising this appendix. Table A-1 presents the data on the income velocity of money for firms by asset size, and Table A-2 presents that for the ratio for government security holdings to bank loans, also for firms by asset size.

TABLE A-1

THE INCOME VELOCITY OF MONEY FOR MANUFACTURING CORPORATIONS BY ASSET SIZE, 1956-63

(Seasonally adjusted[1]—Classes in millions of dollars)

Year and Quarter[2]	Under 1	1 to 5	5 to 10[3]	10 to 25	25 to 50	50 to 100	100 to 250	250 to 1,000	1,000 and over
1956:									
2	5.90	5.38	4.72	4.71		4.35	5.07	5.11	5.46
3	5.91	5.44	4.84	4.76		4.41	5.12	5.22	5.57
4	5.95	5.51	4.89	4.79		4.41	5.20	5.36	5.65
1957:									
1	5.92	5.21	4.94	4.78		4.50	5.21	5.48	5.79
2	5.84	5.56	4.96	4.73		4.53	5.22	5.50	5.81
3(P)	5.73	5.53	4.72	4.59		4.49	5.05	5.60	5.60
4	5.66	5.37	4.39	4.42		4.50	4.89	5.49	5.36
1958:									
1	5.65	5.33	4.14	4.43[4]		4.43	4.82	5.50	5.21
2(T)	5.81	5.23	4.01	4.46	4.22	4.43	4.76	5.55	5.19
3	5.99	5.22	4.07	4.23	4.32	4.45	4.88	5.63	5.40
4	6.18	5.36	4.33	4.24	4.13	4.57	5.12	5.92	5.70
1959:									
1	6.37	5.46	4.63	4.29	4.29	4.70	5.25	6.11	5.82
2	6.45	5.63	4.85	4.57	4.51	4.83	5.39	6.29	5.83
3	6.46	5.77	5.10	4.90	5.12	4.99	5.54	6.47	6.06
4	6.54	5.80	5.31	4.86	5.00	5.12	6.50	6.50	6.21
1960:									
1	6.53	5.82	5.40	4.80	4.98	5.21	5.69	6.59	6.34
2(P)	6.54	5.76	5.41	5.41	5.28	5.20	5.61	6.63	6.41
3	6.47	5.72	5.26	5.61	5.65	5.13	5.52	6.63	6.13
4	6.37	5.77	5.10	5.20	5.30	5.14	5.53	6.74	6.03
1961:									
1(T)	6.26	5.83	5.09	4.89	4.94	5.10	5.60	6.79	6.05
2	6.19	5.89	5.10	5.06	4.99	5.05	5.61	6.69	6.40
3	6.18	5.90	5.20	5.37	5.38	5.20	5.71	6.84	6.82
4	6.15	6.00	5.31	5.20	5.25	5.35	5.76	6.94	7.18
1962:									
1	6.13	6.00	5.43	9.94	5.17	5.56	5.81	7.09	7.38
2	6.08	5.92	5.53	5.33	5.45	5.82	5.80	7.20	7.30
3	6.03	5.94	5.59	5.39	5.63	5.80	5.84	7.22	7.44
4	6.04	5.91	5.67	5.40	5.52	5.78	5.87	7.28	7.57
1963:									
1	6.05	5.95	5.73	5.06	5.41	5.71	5.89	7.26	7.67

1. The seasonal adjustment was effected with a four-quarter moving average.
2. The P's and T's denote quarters in which peaks and troughs occur in the business cycle as reported by the National Bureau of Economic Research.
3. The sample includes all corporations with assets of 5 million dollars and over. For the 1st quarter 1963, this included 1,237 corporations.
4. Prior to 1958, the 10 to 25 million dollars and 25 to 30 million asset size groups were classified as one group.
Sources of data: U. S. Federal Trade Commission and Securities and Exchange Commission.

TABLE A-2

THE RATIO OF GOVERNMENT SECURITY HOLDINGS[1] TO LOANS
FROM BANKS FOR MANUFACTURING CORPORATIONS BY
ASSET SIZE, 1956-63
(Seasonally adjusted[2]—Classes in millions of dollars)

Year and Quarter[3]	Under 1	1 to 5	5 to 10[4]	10 to 25	25 to 50	50 to 100	100 to 250	250 to 1,000	1,000 and over
1956:									
2	0.20	0.37	0.42	0.53		0.93	0.72	1.55	5.09
3	0.19	0.36	0.41	0.46		0.81	0.64	1.25	4.64
4	0.19	0.35	0.41	0.44		0.73	0.59	1.05	4.40
1957:									
1	0.20	0.35	0.42	0.43		0.69	0.55	0.93	4.36
2	0.21	0.35	0.44	0.41		0.67	0.53	0.82	4.38
3(P)	0.22	0.36	0.45	0.43		0.64	0.53	0.74	4.13
4	0.22	0.36	0.45	0.44		0.60	0.55	0.68	4.20
1958:									
1	0.21	0.36	0.46	0.50[5]		0.56	0.56	0.64	4.25
2(T)	0.20	0.35	0.49	0.46	0.50	0.55	0.59	0.66	4.84
3	0.19	0.34	0.53	0.51	0.54	0.56	0.65	0.73	6.07
4	0.18	0.34	0.57	0.57	0.62	0.58	0.74	0.83	7.33
1959:									
1	0.18	0.35	0.57	0.61	0.67	0.62	0.81	0.93	8.48
2	0.18	0.34	0.56	0.62	0.69	0.64	0.86	0.96	8.95
3	0.19	0.35	0.56	0.59	0.66	0.64	0.84	0.92	8.18
4	0.19	0.35	0.53	0.55	0.59	0.63	0.79	0.84	7.20
1960:									
1	0.21	0.34	0.50	0.50	0.52	0.60	0.73	0.74	6.28
2(P)	0.19	0.33	0.47	0.45	0.46	0.57	0.66	0.66	4.59
3	0.18	0.31	0.46	0.44	0.43	0.52	0.60	0.62	5.11
4	0.17	0.30	0.45	0.43	0.43	0.47	0.57	0.61	4.72
1961:									
1(T)	0.15	0.29	0.45	0.43	0.43	0.45	0.55	0.60	4.54
2	0.14	0.27	0.45	0.43	0.44	0.44	0.55	0.60	4.31
3	0.14	0.27	0.42	0.43	0.44	0.44	0.60	0.58	4.35
4	0.14	0.26	0.40	0.42	0.43	0.47	0.65	0.55	4.51
1962:									
1	0.13	0.25	0.38	0.41	0.41	0.47	0.69	0.51	4.54
2	0.13	0.25	0.37	0.39	0.40	0.47	0.70	0.46	4.68
3	0.13	0.24	0.36	0.39	0.38	0.46	0.68	0.47	4.65
4	0.13	0.23	0.36	0.40	0.36	0.46	0.64	0.47	4.61
1963:									
1	0.12	0.23	0.35	0.40	0.34	0.47	0.59	0.49	4.60

1. The category "Government Securities" is described by the data sources as including the "equivalent" of cash on hand. This would, presumabley, include non-cash liquid assets such as time certificates of deposit as well as government securities.

2. The seasonal adjustment was effected with a four-quarter moving average.

3. The P's and T's denote quarters in which peaks and troughs occur in the business cycle as reported by the National Bureau of Economic Research.

4. The sample includes all corporations with assets of 5 million dollars and over. For the 1st quarter 1963, this included 1,237 corporations.

5. Prior to 1958, the 10 to 25 million dollar and 25 to 30 million asset size groups were classified as one group.

Sources of data: U. S. Federal Trade Commission and Securities and Exchange Commission.

8. THE POSTWAR RISE IN THE VELOCITY OF MONEY: ALTERNATIVE VIEWS, THEIR IMPLICATIONS FOR MONETARY POLICY, AND A MACRO MODEL

A number of economists have written about the secular rise in the velocity of money in the United States in the post-World-War-II years with emphasis upon the non-financial business sector. They have placed either a considerable emphasis on this sector or some emphasis on it as a part of the whole economy.[1] In the former of these instances, an examination of secular changes in velocity leads to some conclusions about the contribution of the non-financial business sector to that rise,[2] and/or developments in the business sector are seen as having made a major contribution to the postwar rise in the income velocity of money (i.e., the ratio of gross national product to the total money stock).[3] Earlier (Chap. 1), moreover, such writings were described as belonging to a growing literature that contained elements of both micro- and macro-economic analysis. They were said to "possess the latter elements to one or two extents—to the extent that a connective link is established between the parts and the whole; and/or to the extent that information results so as to contribute to an understanding and/or better prediction of the behavior of the aggregates and the effects of general credit conditions."

This chapter deals briefly with these matters. It contains an outline of the various views concerning the non-financial business sector and the postwar rise in the velocity of money; it deals with the policy implications of the various views; and it contains an outline of an elementary macro model involving the earlier results from analyses of data for firms by asset size, the motives for holding money, the income velocity of money, and other aggregative measures. The results from the earlier statistical analyses are shown to be related to the economy as a whole. Their implications for analysis and policies concerning the economy as a whole are examined.

The model in question has been introduced in two articles,[4] and its macro character is developed in still another source.[5] The elementary model may be viewed against a background of analysis that involves total assets as a constraint, utilizes Legrangian functions, and establishes equi-

1. See, e.g., Selden, "Postwar Rise," p. 531.
2. See Friedman and Schwartz, *Monetary History*, Chap. 12; Frazer, "Monetary Analysis," pp. 584-96.
3. See Ritter, "Structure of Financial Markets," pp. 70-79.
4. Frazer, "Monetary Analysis," pp. 588-90; Frazer, "Some Comments," pp. 76-78.
5. Frazer and Yohe, *Analytics and Institutions*, Secs. 1.2, 2.3, 5.4, 25.4.

librium conditions at a moment in time. The analysis was briefly outlined earlier (Sec. 1.1).

8.1. ALTERNATIVE VIEWS ABOUT THE POSTWAR RISE IN VELOCITY AND THEIR IMPLICATIONS FOR MONETARY POLICY

A policy is a goal, and the monetary officials may be interested in a number of goals such as "free reserves" at the operational level, the stock of money at the intermediate level, and, ultimately, the level of national income.[6] This section, however deals mainly with some aspects of the effects of changes in the stock of money holdings by manufacturing firms. It proceeds by first dealing with the earlier results and the alternative views about the non-financial business sector and the postwar rise in the velocity of money, and then by dealing with the implications of the earlier results and alternative views for several of the possible policies of the monetary or other officials.

Alternative views about the postwar rise in the velocity of money.— Earlier (Sec. 7.3) three sets of circumstances by which most students attempt to explain the postwar rise in the velocity of money were noted. Essentially, the Friedman-Schwartz view involved "a decline in the value attached to monetary services because of changed expectations of holders of money about the likely degree of future economic stability." This was shown to involve a relative decline in the precautionary demand for money balances in the sense that greater certainty about the future reduced the value of the versatility of money and the flexibility it provides for meeting emergencies and for taking advantage of sudden opportunities (Sec. 7.1).

Professor Ritter's view,[7] however, has emphasized the growth of the liquid asset holdings of non-financial corporations and the increased activity of these corporations in the money market, and Professor Selden[8] has concluded that the postwar rise in corporate velocity is not attributable to a shift from cash to government securities. Continuing, Selden notes that, "in fact, non-financial corporate holdings of government securities in 1957 were smaller, relative to cash, than a decade earlier." Also, the postwar decline in the quarterly average for the ratio of government securities to bank loans (Sec. 7.3)—i.e., the index of near moneyness (Sec. 1.1)— and the earlier statement about the relationship between this index and the velocity of money (Sec. 7.2) would indicate that the decline in near moneyness actually operated to offset some of the effects of other forces

---

6. For definitions of the terms "goals" ("targets") and "tools" ("instruments") of monetary policy, see *ibid.*, Secs. 24.1, 24.2.
7. "Structure of Financial Markets," p. 70-79.
8. "Postwar Rise," p. 531.

which contributed to the postwar rise in velocity. Apparently, from among the above views, Ritter's is in the sharpest contrast to the others. It is unsupported by the results from earlier analyses.

Implications for the effects of some policies.—The earlier results have some implications for the effectiveness of credit policies, and there are, in addition, certain lessons to be learned from the effect of postwar monetary developments on the level of expenditures and, therefore, on income and the income velocity of money. With respect to the empirical findings (Sec. 3.1), the tendency for larger firms to place greater emphasis in relation to their asset size on changes in non-cash liquid assets as a means of effecting adjustments in cash needs and the contrasting tendency for the smaller firms to place greater emphasis in relation to their size on bank loans would seem to imply that changes in the cost and availability of credit on business expenditures operate to some degree via different routes. The smaller firms, in relation to their size, would seem to be affected to a greater extent than the larger ones via the availability of bank credit.

Now, the postwar developments would seem to indicate that a rise in the income velocity of money (and, therefore, expenditures) could be accomplished, via a relative weakening of the precautionary motive for holding money, by the creation of an environment in which there is greater certainty about the future. At least, the prospect of a rise for such a reason would not be inconsistent with the facts. This prospect, however, would contrast with the lesson that would follow from Ritter's view. The latter would instead indicate that a rise in the velocity of money of the type in the postwar United States could be accomplished by developing a money market and/or effecting a growth of so-called cash substitutes or money market instruments. An evaluation of these lessons and alternative views may not seem especially important, but they may possibly lead to alternative recommendations to the monetary or policy-making officials. As Professor Rittter has noted, the experience of the United States is "suggestive of the problems likely to be faced by presently undeveloped countries as their financial systems become more complex" and by "advanced economies with highly developed financial systems."[9]

There is, further, an additional implication of the postwar developments in the United States for the effectiveness of monetary policy. There is simply the question of whether the postwar changes in the liquidity structure of firms (or, more specifically, the index of near moneyness) have resulted in an environment that permits some escape from the effectiveness of a tight money policy, or there is the more general question of whether the structural changes have contributed to an increase or decrease in the effectiveness of a given change in the stock of money on the level

9. "Structure of Financial Markets," p. 276.

of income. These questions will be dealt with following the subsequent outline of an elementary monetary model.

8.2. AN ELEMENTARY MODEL: MOTIVES CONCERNING THE PREFERENCE FOR MONEY AND EARLIER STATISTICAL RESULTS

The motives concerning the preference for money include the transactions motive, the speculative motive, and the precautionary motive in both of its earlier senses (Sec. 7.1).[10] Following this division by Keynes, all of the motives are treated as being embodied in the quantity of money demanded as some increasing function of income, and, in addition, the speculative and precautionary motives are related to the conditions underlying this function. The function and the motives are all dealt with in this section in terms of an elementary model. The model is shown to involve earlier empirical findings, the alternative views about the postwar rise in the velocity of money (Sec. 8.1), and some questions concerning the effectiveness of monetary policy. The earlier results are largely from analyses of data for firms by asset size, however, and the model is a macro-economic model. There is the additional need, therefore, to establish some connections between the essentially micro-economic results and the macro model.

The elementary model.—The equations comprising the elementary model are as follows:

$$(1) \quad M_d = \alpha Y + \beta, \, \alpha > 0$$
$$(2) \quad M_s = \gamma$$

Equation (1) defines the quantity of money demanded (M_d) as some increasing linear function of income $(Y \, [= \, GNP])$, given the underlying conditions as represented by the parameters α and β at some given time. It implies that the demand for balances to satisfy each of the motives—transaction, speculative, and precautionary—varies as a function of income (or assets, since income and assets are highly correlated [Sect. 3.1]). A doubling, or increasing by any factor, the level of income (or assets) increases the balances for satisfying the various motives by the same proportion. Changes in the parameter β, then, correspond to changes in the strength of the speculative and/or Friedman-Schwartz precautionary motive for holding money balances (Sec. 7.1). And, next, the changes in α are some decreasing function of near moneyness, and these latter changes involve the precautionary motive in the second of its two senses (Secs. 1.1, 7.1). Proceeding from any base time—i.e., proceeding in the sense of comparative statics—$\beta = 0$ in the above model, and thus $\alpha = M_d/Y$ (i.e., α is initially the reciprocal of the income velocity of money). Equation (2) simply denotes the money supply (M_s)

10. See Keynes, *General Theory*, pp. 170, 195-96; Frazer and Yohe, Secs. 2.2, 4.4.

as some variable constant (γ) since we usually view the money stock as some controlled variable. Clearly, since $\alpha > 0$ and $\gamma = $ constant, a solution exists (i.e., $M_s = M_d$).

Solving the model for income, $Y = (\gamma - \beta)/\alpha$. Here, a weakening of the precautionary motive in relation to the other motives and in its first sense (Sec. 7.1) corresponds to a decline in β and it gives rise to an increase in income. A weakening of the precautionary motive in the second sense (Sec. 7.1) corresponds to a decline in α and so on. Recalling the definition of the income velocity of money (i.e., Y/M), denoting it V_y, substituting our expression for income [i.e., $(\gamma - \beta)/\alpha$], and rearranging terms,

$$(3) \quad V_y = \frac{1 - \beta/\gamma}{\alpha}$$

Thus, velocity, too, varies indirectly with a weakening of the precautionary motive in both of its senses (Sec. 7.1).

A breakdown of the variables of the macro model.—Prior to additional references to the parameters, the variables of the macro model may be broken down into their sectoral components. The stock of money demanded (M_d) may be broken down: $M_d = M_d^{(1)} + M_d^{(2)} + \ldots + M_d^{(n)}$, where $M_d^{(i)}$, $i = 1, \ldots, n$ are the stocks demanded by the n sectors, and $M_d^{(1)}$ is the stock demanded by the money market firms in the FTC-SEC's sample. National income (Y) may be broken down: $Y = Y_1 + Y_2 + \ldots + Y_n$, where Y_i, $i = 1, \ldots, n$ corresponds to the incomes identified with the n respective sectors, and Y_1 corresponds to the income identified with the money market firms. Further, in terms of the above breakdown and the income velocity of money (i.e., $V_y = Y/M_d$),

$$V_y = \frac{Y_1 + Y_2 + \ldots + Y_n}{M_d^{(1)} + M_d^{(2)} + \ldots + M_d^{(n)}}$$

$$V_y^{(i)} = \frac{Y_i}{M_d^{(i)}} \quad i = 1, \ldots, n,$$

$$V_y^{(1)} = \frac{Y_1}{M_d^{(1)}},$$

and instead of dealing with changes in the latter measure of velocity,[10a] one may use changes in the ratio of sales to cash as a substitute measure (Sec. 7.2).

The parameter α.—With reference to definition (3),

$$(4) \quad \alpha = f(L_1, L_2, \ldots, L_n) \text{ and } \frac{\partial \alpha}{\partial L_1} < 0$$

10a. On the relationship between sector velocities ($V_y^{(1)}$ in the present case), aggregate velocity (V_y) and the method of computing weights to determine the relative importance of sector velocities, see Selden, *Postwar Rise*, note 11, pp. 489-90.

where L's are indexes of near moneyness for the n different sectors of the economy, and L_1 is the index of near moneyness (i.e., the ratio of government security holdings to bank loans) for the manufacturing firm with assets of 17.5 million dollars and over.

Above, one notes that as L_1 increases, α declines, and, given definition (3), V_y increases. Also, income ($= GNP$) increases, given $Y = (\gamma - \beta)/\alpha$ as a solution to equations (1) and (2). This phenomenon is a weakening of the precautionary motive of the first type (Secs. 1.1, 3.1, and 7.1 in particular). The balances get released to government securities and the turnover of the remaining balances increases by definition (3). Simply changing the scale of operations leads one to expect $\partial\alpha/\partial L_1 = 0$, since the ratio of government securities to bank loans does not change under such scale changes (Sec. 1.2). But the functional relationship (4), whereby $\partial\alpha/\partial L_1 < 0$, is established by the results of statistical analyses as reported in Tables 7-1, 7-2, and 5-3.

The parameter β.—Changes in β are not dealt with in terms of empirical findings, although they enter into the model. Changes in β are simply noted as being associated (1) with shifts in the relative strength of that portion of the precautionary motive dealing with certainty about the future, and/or (2) with some switching of assets with a fixed claim against future income (or GNP) in current prices, such as money balances vis-à-vis assets with a residual claim against future income in current prices such as plant and equipment.

Of course, $\Delta\beta$ could be viewed as being a function of changes in the various sectors, just as α above. In such a case,

$$\Delta\beta = f(F_1, F_2, \ldots, F_n), \quad \frac{\partial\Delta\beta}{\partial F_1} > 0$$

where F's correspond to cash balances (as a proportion of assets) with fixed claims against future income, and F_1 corresponds to the proportion of cash the money market firms (Sec. 7.2) wish to hold. As an aside, one may note that $\Delta F_1/\Delta t < 0$ in the expansion phase of a cycle and $\Delta F_1/\Delta t > 0$ in the contraction phase, since changes in time (Δt) are always positive and $\Delta F_1 < 0$ in expansion phase and $\Delta F_1 > 0$ in the contraction phase.[10b]

10b. As the latter sub-section of the text suggests, and apart from the role of the precautionary motive, the present elementary model (along with its more elaborate development, see note 4, above) contains many of the elements of Meltzer's demand function for money ("Demand for Money," pp. 407-8). The similarity is particularly evident with respect to several features: the role of shifts in cash as a proportion of assets when there is some imbalance between the rate of return on physical capital and the rate of interest, the inverse change in the proportion of assets with a residual claim against future income, and the velocity of money. These elements are not written into a single demand equation but they enter indirectly into the expression for the velocity of money via the motives for holding money. In the Meltzer

The rationale of splitting the precautionary motive(s).—In reviewing several aspects of earlier sections, the rationale of splitting the precautionary motive(s) between the parameters α and β may be shown to involve a use of econometric theory and the earlier (Sec. 7.1) definition(s) of the precautionary motive(s). It is also consistent with analyses of data.

The econometric theory involved concerns Valavanis' point that statistical estimates of demand relationships from cross section and time series data do not involve different kinds of behavior.[11] The point permits us to use cross section data to establish a functional relationship which we deal with in terms of changes over time. Next, if one views structural changes of the type involving the ratio of government securities to bank loans (i.e., shifts in α) as occurring coincidentally over time with any possible parallel shifts in the demand function for money (i.e., shifts in β), then the actual changes in the holdings of money balances in relation to the shifts in β produce a smaller multiplier effect as α increases (i.e., the index of near money decreases), and a larger multiplier effect as cash gets transferred into income or expenditures via a decrease in α (i.e., increasing near moneyness). The only way this combination of changes can be shown in a model of the above type is by splitting the precautionary motive(s) between slope and intercept parameters. The demonstration of the changes above, moreover, is consistent with empirical results as reviewed below.

The Friedman-Schwartz explanation and a secular decline in the index of near moneyness.—The major emphasis in the Friedman-Schwartz explanation of the postwar rise in velocity (Sec. 7.3) is in terms of a secular decline in β, and this decline in β gives rise to an increase in velocity by the definitional equation (3). Secular changes reported earlier (Sec. 7.3), however, indicate that the index of near moneyness declined, and thus the changes reported earlier indicate an increase in α since α is a decreasing function of the index by equation (4) and since the index declined. The postwar changes in the financial structure of firms as indicated by the changes in the index, consequently, actually tended to reduce velocity.

---

framework, the function f (S, r, ρ, K) may be viewed as denoting the demand for money (M), where the following hold: S is sales, r is the market rate of interest, ρ is the internal yield (as a rate) to the firm, changes in K correspond directly to changes in the ratio of capital to labor,

$$\frac{dM/M}{dS/S} = 1, \quad \frac{dM}{d\rho} \quad \text{and} \quad \frac{dM}{dr} < 0, \quad \frac{dF_1}{dK} \gtrless 0$$

in the expansion and contraction phases respectively (F_1, as defined in the text.) In both the model of Sec. 8.2 and the Meltzer function, changes in internal and market yields parallel inverse changes in cash as a percentage of assets, direct changes in productive capital as a percentage of assets, and direct changes in velocity.

11. *Econometrics*, pp. 192-96.

For the present purposes, these facts mean several things. For one, there is more of a postwar rise in velocity to be explained with respect to the non-financial business sector than Friedman and Schwartz thought. For another, the results as noted elsewhere,[12] are "contrary to the Ritter explanation in terms of government securities and the growth of a highly developed money market."

The secular change in near moneyness and the effectiveness of monetary policy.—The secular decline in the ratio of government securities to bank loans (Sec. 7.3) suggests that the slope parameter in equation (1) increased over the postwar years. In other words, the liquidity structure (Sec. 3.1) of firms changed so that the slope of the demand function for money increased (i.e., dM_d/dY increased or α increased). This means that a given change in income would cause the quantity of money demanded to rise more in 1960, for example, than in 1948. At least this would be so as far as the structural changes involving near moneyness for the manufacturing firms in question are concerned (Sec. 7.3). To put the question another way, would a given percentage change in the money stock call forth a smaller or larger percentage change in income in 1960 than in 1948? Denoting such a change $\dfrac{\Delta Y/Y}{\Delta M/M}$ or $\dfrac{\partial Y}{\partial \gamma} \dfrac{\gamma}{Y}$ the crucial factor becomes $\partial Y/\partial \gamma$. Thus, differentiating income [i.e., $Y = (\gamma - \beta)/\alpha$] with respect to the stock of money $\partial Y/\partial \gamma = 1/\alpha$ and the change denoted above in income in response to a change in the stock of money becomes less as α increases. This means, among other things, that postwar changes in firms' liquidity structure did not in themselves result in an environment that permitted an escape from a tight money policy via a greater rise in the velocity of money.

The elementary model and results from cross section data.—Note, in terms of the elementary model and cross section data (Sec. 7.2) what the model predicts as firms increase in size beyond some minimum. In terms of statements 1 to 3 (Sec. 7.2) the index of near moneyness increases (i.e., α decreases in the present model) and this in turn contributes to a rise in velocity. Thus, there is some empirical support for the capacity of the model to predict changes that are consistent with empirical findings (Sec. 7.2), an earlier proposition, and the corollary to the proposition (Sec. 1.1). The earlier logical results indicate that the precautionary demand does not increase proportionally with wealth and that its failure to do so contributes to an increase in the turnover of cash balances. At least this is true insofar as the corporate manufacturing sector is concerned.

---

12. Frazer, "Monetary Analysis," pp. 584-96.

8.3. SUMMARY

A number of economists have written about the postwar rise in the velocity of money in the United States with some emphasis on the contribution of the non-financial business sector to that rise. The view of one of these economists—Professor Ritter—was that the growth in the government security holdings of large corporations provided an enlarged pool of near money assets and that the extra moneyness, in turn, released balances to the more active transactions sphere. Richard T. Selden disputed such a claim on empirical grounds, and our own findings indicated that near moneyness in relation to assets and sales (or income) did not increase. Indeed, as a fact, the ratio of government security holdings to bank loans declined and this decline in the ratio was shown to have exercised a damping effect on velocity.

Friedman and Schwartz, on the other hand, explained the postwar rise in the velocity of money in terms of a greater certainty about the future and need to hold relatively smaller balances for meeting emergencies and taking advantage of unforeseen opportunities. They extended this explanation to include the non-financial business sector, in particular, and this view was shown to be consistent with the present findings and analysis. The analysis of the relationship between the velocity of cash balances (i.e., the ratio of sales to cash) and the ratio of government security holdings to bank loans, however, indicated the need to explain more than the apparent rise in velocity.

The alternative views have some interesting implications for actions by public officials. The Ritter view could lead public officials to attempt to effect a rise in velocity, as in the postwar United States, by increasing the volume of money market instruments. The Friedman-Schwartz view could lead them to attempt to bring about a more certain outlook about the future on the part of the investors and managers of corporate funds.

Another policy implication, one resulting from the decline in the ratio of government security holdings to bank loans, is that a given change in corporate cash would be accompanied by a smaller turnover of cash in the later than in the earlier postwar years. At least this implication would follow as far as postwar changes in near moneyness alone were concerned.

Still another implication—one concerning changes in the liquidity structure of firms by asset size—for the effects of credit ease or tightness is that these effects operate on different asset size groups via different routes. The larger firms would seem to be affected to a greater extent than the smaller firms by conditions in the financial markets generally. The smaller firms would seem to be affected to a greater extent than the larger ones by the availability of bank credit.

Finally, given the quantity of cash as some increasing linear function of income, such as would result from a simple increase in the scale of operation, slope and intercept parameters, respectively, were viewed as being related to different aspects of the precautionary motive for holding cash. The intercept parameter was viewed as varying directly with changes in one aspect of the precautionary demand, namely, that involving the outlook toward the future and the possible need for cash to meet emergencies and take advantage of unforeseen opportunities. The slope parameter was viewed as varying directly with a second aspect of the precautionary demand for balances relative to other demands. This was that part involving balances to meet liabilities fixed in terms of money such as bank loans or, more specifically, the slope parameter was viewed as a decreasing function of the ratio of government securities to bank loans. This demand function for money, in combination with a supply function, was viewed as comprising an elementary model. The model was then viewed in relation to the present statistical analyses and it was shown to generate the sort of result that followed from the recognition of the two aspects of the precautionary motive and the various empirical findings.

9. SUMMARY

The present study of the demand for money, bank loans, and government securities involves changes that occur in the financial structure of manufacturing corporations in relation to their classification by asset size. In particular, tests of data concerning two propositions are reported. The principal among these is that the type 2 precautionary demand for money balances does not increase proportionally with asset size (and presumably income or sales). This type 2 demand concerns mainly the relationship between money balances and bank loans. The corollary to the proposition is that the turnover of the cash balances held by manufacturing corporations increases as the firms in question increase in size beyond some minimum and over the predominant portion of the asset size scale over which asset sizes actually vary. To provide empirical support for the propositions, data are tested concerning statements about selected asset and other accounts and, therefore, changes in the financial structure of manufacturing firms.

The data tested are, for the most part, those for manufacturing corporations as reported by the FTC-SEC. There are special features about our uses of the data that call for comment. For one, the treatment of classes of assets and liabilities as percentages of total assets (or the treatment of ratios expressed as percentages) in relation to asset size results in our dependent variables being independent of the dollar volume of assets in a given class. For another, the use of these various percentages in relation to relatively much larger magnitudes for asset size makes it difficult to determine whether straight lines or curves provide the best fit to the respective sets of points for the relationships in question, and there are other problems as well in the use of FTC-SEC data, especially with respect to their use as precise quantitative measures of changes over time. For the latter reasons, and in order to present the results of some tests of data, linear regression lines have been used as first approximations to the various relationships, and the analysis has, for the most part, been viewed as a qualitative analysis.

Income statements and balance sheets serve as sources of data. Retained earnings net of taxes, as shown on the income statement, are a source of corporate funds; and the ratio of retained earnings to earnings net of taxes serves as a measure of the relative importance of retained earnings for firms in different asset size groups. Any increase (decrease) in the accounts on the asset side of the balance sheets serves as a use (source) of funds, and any increase (decrease) in the accounts on the liabilities and net worth side as a source (use) of funds. In both instances, all sources and uses of funds revolve about the cash account, but the principal accounts reflecting the capacity of enterprises to effect expenditures on short notice are those for cash, government or other liquid securities, and bank loans. The liquidity ratio involves these accounts, and serves as a means of dealing with possible differences between the capacity of firms of different asset sizes to effect expenditures on short notice, in relation to asset size and independent of the dollar volume of assets in each asset size group.

The principal accounts reflecting the capacity of firms to obtain cash on short notice are government or similar liquid securities and bank loans. The ratio of these two accounts, consequently, serves as an indicator of near moneyness. It is also a means of dealing with the differences with respect to the near moneyness of varying asset size groups, again in relation to asset size and independent of the dollar volume of assets in each asset size group.

The statistical findings indicate that bank loans and cash as percentages of assets decline as firms increase in size. These findings, in combination with that of a near-perfect direct relationship between income (sales) and wealth (assets), support the proposition that the type 2 precautionary demand for money rises less than proportionally with wealth or income (or sales). The results of linear approximations reveal, furthermore, a tendency for money balances as a percentage of assets to be transferred to securities and, given this tendency, the decline in bank loans contributes to a rise in liquidity in response to increasing asset size.

85

These latter findings are important for various reasons: Contemporary writers in the monetary area have been inclined to overlook certain aspects of the precautionary motive for holding money in their analyses and, somewhat along the same line, the findings indicate a need to examine certain prevailing views in contemporary monetary literature. There are other instances where one element of the precautionary demand for money, as defined earlier, has been overlooked, but one of these concerns the view that money is a luxury good. In contrast to this view, there is empirical support for the proposition that the precautionary demand rises less than proportionally with wealth (assets) and for the assumed relationship between wealth and income (or sales). This proposition and the relationship suggest that the ratio of sales to money balances must be rising, at least over some major portion of the domain over which asset sizes actually vary.

The pattern of changes in the accounts for bank loans and government securities lends empirical support to the possible significance of earlier suggestions that were thought to be lurking behind the changes in the financial structure. In particular, the tendency for bank loans as a percentage of assets to decline foretells the presence of a relatively weak relationship between changes in inventories and the use of bank credit as a source of funds.

The results from linear approximations to data and tests concerning changes in the financial structure in relation to asset size indicate that the overall changes in the financial structure mainly reflect the changes in the liquidity structure. As opposed to the changes noted in the liquidity structure, linear approximations to relationships and tests of data suggest that the following are relatively independent of asset size: the ratio of accounts receivable to accounts payable, retained earnings as a percentage of net earnings, long-term debt as a percentage of assets, and owners' equity as a percentage of assets.

The tendency for bank loans as a percentage of assets to decline leads us to examine certain of the aspects of the commercial loan doctrine. That doctrine held, among some other things, that commercial banks should confine their lending activities to short-term, self-liquidating, commercial loans. This doctrine had its impact on the writing of the original Federal Reserve Act, and on economic analysis. In the latter case, it led to the view that apparent parallel movements in bank loans and inventories reflected a use of bank loans as a means of financing inventories. As matters have evolved, the Federal Reserve Act has changed, and no economist or operating banker would expect a commercial bank to adhere to the stringent rules of the early doctrine. Some, nevertheless, have thought of changes in bank loans as a predominant source of funds for effecting the purchase of inventories in the short run and, in any event, there has been a scarcity of satisfactory tests of data concerning the relationship between changes in bank loans and inventory changes.

To deal more thoroughly with the latter relationship, the relevant data for nine classes of manufacturing corporations were analyzed. The results support our view. Changes in bank loans are an increasing function of changes in inventories but, even in this case, the slopes for the linear approximations to the data for the different asset size classes are significantly different from zero for less than half of the asset size classes. Any formal statement about a parallel movement in time series for bank loans and inventories for the various asset size classes is largely without empirical support.

What may appear as parallel movements in series for some aggregates for bank loans and inventories should not be interpreted as a use of bank loans for financing short-run increases in inventories. Small portions of funds from both short- and long-term bank loans may be used to purchase inventories, but the experience concerning even the use of these small portions of bank funds by different asset size groups is quite diverse. For a given increase in inventories, some asset size classes will use bank loans as a source of financing to more than twice the extent of other classes by asset size, as indicated by the respective slopes of our linear approximations.

The sort of criticism made about the tendency to view bank loans as a major source of funds for effecting expenditures on inventories leads us to examine Professor Bloch's analysis of the demand for money and government securities. In particular, his analysis emphasizes a special category called "free governments"—i.e., government security holdings net of tax liabilities. He then proceeds to view the government security holdings in this category as the major means of effecting adjustments in the cash account. Among other things, he views this pool of liquid assets as being related to "unknown future investment outlays." Our statistical analyses indicate, however, that the emphasis on a special category called "free governments" is without satisfactory empirical foundation and that, contrary to Bloch's assertion, firms' pools of liquidity have some relationship to planned capital outlays. Our review of his approach within the context of a sources-and-uses-of-funds framework indicates, too, that he would have been just as warranted in emphasizing changes in loans as a source of liquidity as "free governments."

Bloch failed to deal explicitly with bank loans as an important means of effecting adjustments in the cash account and as a factor affecting the demand for cash. Bank loans, in particular, have been referred to by Professor Timberlake as a "neglected" factor in analyses of the demand for money, but changes in indebtedness at the bank have been emphasized in the present approach to firms' demands for money. Timberlake, nevertheless, is critical of the role attributed to so-called money substitutes in monetary theory and policy. The present statistical findings, on the other hand, are consistent with that portion of Keynesian theory in which increasing near moneyness diminishes "the demand for money proper and increases the velocity of circulation."

There is strong overall support for our general approach to firms' demands for money, government securities, and bank loans. This approach emphasizes the prevalence of a pool of liquidity that is affected by liquid asset holdings, bank loans, and the strength of the various motives for holding money. In particular, there is an apparent tendency for certain aspects of the precautionary demand for money balances to increase less than proportionally as asset size increases. This is apparently reflected in the additional tendency for the income velocity of money (i.e., the ratio of sales to cash in the present instance) to rise as firms begin to effect a sizable portion of cash adjustments through the money market.

The present emphasis is upon certain aspects of firms' demands for money, bank loans, and government securities. This is, in part, because of the role of liquidity in monetary economics, and it is, in part, because the analyses of data showed these accounts to vary more in relation to changes in asset size. Nevertheless, other accounts may serve as a source or use of money balance and exercise some effect on the turnover of such balances, and, as a consequence, they may be of interest to those who wish to deal with the effectiveness of changes in the stock of money on expenditures. In particular, some research by Allan Meltzer has focused upon such changes, and portions of Meltzer's reports on the research appear on the surface to conflict, primarily, with the results from linear approximations to cross section data for the ratio of accounts receivable to accounts payable and firms by asset size. They also appear to conflict, to a lesser extent, with present notions about the relative independence of large firms from banks.

Meltzer's work on trade credit focuses upon changes in the ratio of net receivables (i.e., receivables less payables) to sales for the manufacturing sector as a means of dealing with a number of questions—some about the possible discriminatory effect of general credit controls on small firms, and some about the allocation and redistribution of bank credit via changes in the ratio of net receivables to sales. Meltzer arrives at a number of conclusions: Small firms are net receivers of trade credit from large firms during periods of tight money; the drain on cash by the increase in net receivables for large firms contributes to a rise in the turnover of their money balances; changes in the velocity of money balances serve to redistribute new and existing money balances in favor of the smaller firms; and the redistribution effect of changes in velocity or, more directly, changes in net receivables must be allowed for in assessing the impact of a tight money policy.

The conflict between the Meltzer conclusions and the present findings, however, are more apparent than real. Taking an overall view—making allowances for both the data originally at Meltzer's disposal and later results from cross section data—the redistribution effects via net receivables appear to work mainly through the relationships between manufacturing firms and wholesale and retail firms rather than within the corporate manufacturing sector. The tendency for the mass of wholesale and retail firms to be small relative to manufacturing firms should not obscure the fact that the Meltzer process applies mainly to relationships between the corporate manufacturing sector and the sectors receiving its products rather than between firms in the corporate manufacturing sector itself. In order to assess more fully the impact of tight money on the various sectors and, thus, ultimately the impact (Sec. 8.2) upon national income, the level of employment, and the average of prices, one must examine, among other things, changes in the financial structure of the units comprising the various sectors and their responses to changes in the stock of money.

The earlier suggestion whereby the income velocity of money rises as firms begin to effect a portion of adjustments through the money market is in contrast to the Friedman-Schwartz view of money as a "luxury" good for non-financial business firms. By money's being a "luxury" good, they mean that the velocity of money declines as wealth increases. They hold this view, both with respect to the entire economy and with respect to the non-financial business sector. Present findings, however, do not support this view, as it applies to the corporate manufacturing sector. Instead, they show that the ratio of sales to cash varies directly with asset size (and sales), at least as asset size (and sales) increase beyond some minimum size.

To deal empirically with the question of money's being a "luxury" good, a number of steps were taken: Linear approximations were made to data concerning the various relationships, and a proposition was presented. The proposition emphasized that money balances are drawn into the more active transactions sphere as firms increase in asset size. This phenomenon was related to the precautionary motive for holding money balances. The various linear approximations to cross section data, slope parameters, and coefficients of determination, all taken together, indicate the following, for asset sizes in excess of 17.5 million dollars: (1) velocity (sales/cash) varies directly with asset size (and presumably income); (2) asset size varies directly with sales (or income), and, for large firms in general, an increase in assets results in an equal increase in sales; (3) the ratio of government securities to bank loans, as a measure of near moneyness, varies directly with asset size; and (4) velocity varies directly with the latter measure for near moneyness.

The first and second of the statements in the latter list and the tests of data pertaining to both statements support the view whereby the amount of money demanded rises less than in proportion to the rise in asset size. The entire list of statements supports the above proposition, including the claim about the relevance of the precautionary motive. Friedman and Schwartz, moreover, are said to overlook the relevance of the ratio of government securities to bank loans in explaining the post-war rise in velocity. This ratio is shown to have offset some of the rise that would have occurred had the ratio remained constant. Thus, there is more than the apparent increase in velocity to be explained.

Milton Friedman and Anna Jacobson Schwartz, among other econo-mists, have also written about the postwar rise in the velocity of money in the United States with some emphasis on the contribution of the non-financial business sector to that rise. The view of one of these econo-mists—Professor Ritter—was that the growth in the government security holdings of large corporations provided an enlarged pool of near money assets and that the extra moneyness, in turn, released balances to the more active transactions sphere. Another, Richard T. Selden, disputed such a claim on empirical grounds, and the present findings indicate that near moneyness in relation to assets and sales (or income) did not increase. Indeed, as a fact, the ratio of government security holdings to bank loans declined and this decline in the ratio was shown to have exercised a damping effect on velocity.

Friedman and Schwartz, on the other hand, explained the postwar rise in the velocity of money in terms of a greater certainty about the future and the need to hold relatively fewer balances for meeting emergencies and taking advantage of unforeseen opportunities. They extended this ex-planation to include the non-financial business sector, in particular, and this view was shown to be consistent with the present empirical findings and analyses. The analysis of the relationship between the velocity of cash balances (i.e., the ratio of sales to cash) and the ratio of government se-curity holdings to bank loans, however, indicated the need to explain more than the apparent rise in velocity.

The alternative views about the postwar rise in the velocity of money have some interesting implications for actions by public officials. The Rit-ter view could lead public officials to attempt to effect a rise in velocity, as in the postwar United States, by increasing the volume of money mar-ket instruments. The Friedman-Schwartz view would lead them to attempt to bring about a more certain outlook about the future on the part of the investors and managers of corporate funds.

Another policy implication, one resulting from the secular decline in the ratio of government security holdings to bank loans, was that a given change in corporate cash would have a smaller effect on the turnover of cash in the later vis-à-vis earlier postwar years. At least this implication would follow as far as postwar changes in near moneyness alone were concerned. The implication would also be in contrast to the view that postwar changes in the liquidity of corporate manufacturing firms had provided an escape from the effects of a tight credit policy.

Still another implication—one concerning changes in the liquidity structure of firms by asset size—for the effects of credit ease or tightness is that these effects operate on different asset size groups via different routes. The larger firms would seem to be affected to a greater extent than the smaller firms via the conditions in the financial markets generally. The smaller firms would seem to be affected to a greater extent than the larger ones via the availability of bank credit.

Finally, given the quantity of cash as some increasing linear function of income, such as would result from a simple increase in the scale of operation, slope and intercept parameters, respectively, were viewed as being related to separate aspects of the precautionary motive for holding cash. The intercept parameter in particular was viewed as varying directly with changes in one aspect of the precautionary demand relative to other demands. This aspect of the precautionary demand was that involving the outlook toward the future and the possible need for cash to meet emergencies and take advantage of unforeseen opportunities.

The slope parameter was viewed as varying directly with a second aspect of the precautionary demand for balances relative to other demands. This was that part involving balances to meet liabilities fixed in terms of money such as bank loans or, in other words, the slope parameter was viewed as some decreasing function of the ratio of government securities to bank loans.

This linear demand function for money, in combination with a supply function, was viewed as comprising an elementary model. The model, then, was viewed in relation to our statistical analyses and it was shown to generate the same sort of results that followed from the recognition of the two aspects of the precautionary motive and the various empirical findings.

UNIVERSITY OF FLORIDA MONOGRAPHS

Social Sciences

No. 1 (Winter 1959): *The Whigs of Florida, 1845-1854*. By Herbert J. Doherty, Jr.

No. 2 (Spring 1959): *Austrian Catholics and the Social Question, 1918-1933*. By Alfred Diamant

No. 3 (Summer 1959): *The Siege of St. Augustine in 1702*. By Charles W. Arnade

No. 4 (Fall 1959): *New Light on Early and Medieval Japanese Historiography*. By John A. Harrison

No. 5 (Winter 1960): *The Swiss Press and Foreign Affairs in World War II*. By Frederick H. Hartmann

No. 6 (Spring 1960): *The American Militia: Decade of Decision, 1789-1800*. By John K. Mahon

No. 7 (Summer 1960): *The Foundation of Jacques Maritain's Political Philosophy*. By Hwa Yol Jung

No. 8 (Fall 1960): *Latin American Population Studies*. By T. Lynn Smith

No. 9 (Winter 1961): *Jacksonian Democracy on the Florida Frontier*. By Arthur W. Thompson

No. 10 (Spring 1961): *Holman Versus Hughes: Extension of Australian Commonwealth Powers*. By Conrad Joyner

No. 11 (Summer 1961): *Welfare Economics and Subsidy Programs*. By Milton Z. Kafoglis

No. 12 (Fall 1961): *Tribune of the Slavophiles: Konstantin Aksakov*. By Edward Chmielewski

No. 13 (Winter 1962): *City Managers in Politics: An Analysis of Manager Tenure and Termination*. By Gladys M. Kammerer, Charles D. Farris, John M. DeGrove, and Alfred B. Clubok

No. 14 (Spring 1962): *Recent Southern Economic Development as Revealed by the Changing Structure of Employment*. By Edgar S. Dunn, Jr.

No. 15 (Summer 1962): *Sea Power and Chilean Independence*. By Donald E. Worcester

No. 16 (Fall 1962): *The Sherman Antitrust Act and Foreign Trade*. By Andre Simmons

No. 17 (Winter 1963): *The Origins of Hamilton's Fiscal Policies*. By Donald F. Swanson

No. 18 (Spring 1963): *Criminal Asylum in Anglo-Saxon Law*. By Charles H. Riggs, Jr.

No. 19 (Summer 1963): *Colonia Barón Hirsch, A Jewish Agricultural Colony in Argentina*. By Morton D. Winsberg

No. 20 (Fall 1963): *Time Deposits in Present-Day Commercial Banking*. By Lawrence L. Crum

No. 21 (Winter 1964): *The Eastern Greenland Case in Historical Perspective*. By Oscar Svarlien

No. 22 (Spring 1964): *Jacksonian Democracy and the Historians*. By Alfred A. Cave

No. 23 (Summer 1964): *The Rise of the American Chemistry Profession, 1850-1900*. By Edward H. Beardsley

No. 24 (Fall 1964): *Aymara Communities and the Bolivian Agrarian Reform*. By William E. Carter

No. 25 (Winter 1965): *Conservatives in the Progressive Era: The Taft Republicans of 1912*. By Norman M. Wilensky

No. 26 (Spring 1965): *The Anglo-Norwegian Fisheries Case of 1951 and the Changing Law of the Territorial Sea*. By Teruo Kobayashi

No. 27 (Summer 1965): *The Liquidity Structure of Firms and Monetary Economics*. By William J. Frazer, Jr.